JEWISH GAME CHANGERS

By Diane A. McNeil

Copyright © 2011 by Diane A. McNeil

Jewish Game Changers
by Diane A. McNeil

Printed in the United States of America

ISBN 9781619963825

All rights reserved solely by the author. The author guarantees all contents are original and do not infringe upon the legal rights of any other person or work. No part of this book may be reproduced in any form without the permission of the author. The views expressed in this book are not necessarily those of the publisher.

Unless otherwise indicated, Bible quotations are taken from *King James Open Bible (Authorized King James Version), 1985,* by Thomas Nelson, Inc.

www.xulonpress.com

Dedication

To My Grandchildren

My precious ones, I feel it is important to know one's spiritual heritage, and I wanted you to hear this particular segment from me. In the beginning I set out to write these true accounts so that you would know the amazing adventures of your plain and simple "Gramma" and God's Chosen People, the Jews. However, the more I wrote, the more I realized that this is not an ordinary journey; it is far too important to keep in the family.

These incidents span more than thirty years and have uniquely woven my Christian world into the six thousand year old world of Judaism. This is a message for all who truly love God. Everyone with listening ears should understand the great lengths to which our Lord will go to pursue unity between Jews and Christians, and that He will use anyone who dares join Him in this pursuit.

If I could pass along one thing to you other than loving the Lord God with all your heart, soul, mind and strength, it would be an unconditional love for Israel and the Jewish people.

So, it is to you, my dearest grandchildren, that I dedicate *Jewish Game Changers* and pray that one day you, too, will have your own exploits – stories of great adventure and intrigue – in your personal quest for unity between the Church and the Chosen. I love you dearly, Gramma.

Acknowledgments

There would be no game changer without God ordaining it so. He is First and Foremost, and He is the Game Changer in the first two chapters. How appropriate that this journey should begin with Him.

I wish I felt at liberty to acknowledge by name each of the Jewish game changers God used to showcase His favored agenda of Jewish-Christian relations, but I have chosen rather to use fictitious names to protect their identities, except where the individuals' stories have been publically recorded. For the others: You know who you are, and I want to say a personal word to each of you. Chapter Three: A. – How I love you! Thank you for always being yourself and for allowing the Lord to use you to effect the lives of many. Chapter Four: G. – the great teacher and one highly esteemed. Thank you, Lord, for his incredible legacy! Chapter Five: N. – You have profoundly enriched my life! Without you, there would be very few of these episodes. I am deeply indebted to you for a lifetime of service which I will gladly repay. I love you with an everlasting love. Chapter Six: G. – instigator in the founding of Christian Friends of Israel, Memphis – what a bridge builder this little organization has been, and what insight and sensitivity to God's leading on your part. Chapter Seven: the Jewish Memorial Booklets God provided as our guide for fund raising for our Christian project – What an incredible demonstration of His love! Truly amazing! Chapter Eight: N. – whom God used to brilliantly and biblically explain the true meaning of conversion. Chapter Nine: the unnamed Orthodox Rabbi who not only took my breath away by declaring that his son was not the Messiah, but who gave me a greater sensitivity to Judaism. Chapter Ten: N. and M. – for their affirmation of my eating kosher. You will never know how God has used you to positively impact my life. Chapter Eleven: N. – for insisting that I pursue the pardon. Wisdom abounds in you, my dearest friend! Chapter Twelve: J. – the Mother of the Bat Mitzvah daughter who allowed our home to be used for their special Shabbat meal. You know I love you. Thank you for gracing our home that appointed evening. Chapter Thirteen: Nina, Henrietta and Max – beloved and compassionate Holocaust survivors who agreed to be interviewed for *The Remembering*. You hold the dearest places in all our hearts. We love you more than words can express. Chapter Fourteen: Dee – who discovered that she is a Sephardic Jew. Thank you, Father, for allowing me to have a part in this discovery; and, thank you, Dee, for your obedience in writing the Endorsement for *Ruth 3,000 Years of Sleeping Prophecy*. Chapter Fifteen: J. and S. (the two Jewish members of our Israel Prayer Group) – Oh, how we all love you and feel that you make our circle complete. To J. in particular – We love your comedian side; never stop. Laughter is such good medicine. Chapter Sixteen: Michael Swartz – artist on the *Unknown Child* Holocaust Pennies Project, We cannot wait to see what God has decreed will be birthed through this assignment. How thrilling it is to be part of this marvelous adventure! Chapter Seventeen: A., my favorite Jewish game changer chef – Neither of us could ever have known what the Lord was up to that fateful night. He certainly blessed! I thank my God upon every remembrance of you. Chapter Eighteen: the unnamed Rabbi for illustrating unconditional love, and the Gentile funeral attendee who unashamedly demonstrated "hands-on" unconditional love at the funeral of M., where I and every Jewish person present were provoked to jealousy. Thank you, Lord, for that insightful teaching.

Much of this material is either directly or indirectly related to our Christian Friends of Israel, Memphis group. Many have come and gone during the course of our existence, and others have remained constants. But each has had an integral role to play. It has been an honor to have been a part of this organization whose sole purpose is to bless the Memphis and Mid-South Jewish Community. What a privilege to serve with you: Ann Abeln, Annah Brower, Ira Bush, Edith L. Crook, Emily Jo Greer, George King, John R. Mays, Ken McNeil, Ruth Overton, June Purnell, Sue Richmond, Jay R. Robinson, Donna Sularin, Janie Twaddle, Jon Walker, Mary Jane Walker, Frank Webb and Sandra Webb. We serve for no other reward than to hear, "Well done, good and faithful servant."

To the Israel Prayer Group: I love each of you, my dear sisters in the Lord, and praise God for knitting our lives together – for Israel's sake: A., C., C., C., D., E., G., J., S. and S. I also thank you for praying over these game changers.

To Ken, my devoted husband: We have seen a lot during our nearly fifty years of marriage, been through our share of difficulties, bickered a little, but always loved in the good times and the bad. I cannot imagine this game changer journey without your constant love and support – whether or not you understood. Never at any time has your love for me ever wavered. I am so humbled by your unfaltering love and your selflessness to all our family. All praise to God for His unspeakable gifts!

To my dear friends who agreed to read the manuscript for content, input, feedback, etc., my heart overflows with thanksgiving. You knew I genuinely needed your help. How can I ever express my gratitude? Sincerest thanks to Beverly, Gloria, Judy, Kathryn, Mary Jane, Nancy, Pat, Peggy, Rebecca and the entire Israel prayer group.

Finally, to my beloved cousin Wanda, journalist and author – Thank you for the many hours editing this work. You were right: I did see more red ink than I had ever seen in my life. What a difference a professional makes. Thank you for embracing this project and for the many words of encouragement. May God repay you richly from His vast storehouse.

Table of Contents

Dedication 5

Acknowledgments 7

Introduction 13

1. A Glimpse into God's Secret Place 17
2. My Ruth Encounter 22
3. A Birthday Surprise 28
4. Ask and Ye Shall Receive 33
5. The Lone Gentile in Hebrew Class 39
6. The Open Door 45
7. God's Approach to Fundraising 52
   Picture of Ambulance Door 58
   Fundraising Booklet 59
8. Elvis's Love for the Jews … and More 60
9. A Visit with the Rabbi 68
10. A New Twist on Kosher 72
11. The Pardon 80
   Governor's Letter of Pardon 87

12. A Christian and the Sabbath 88

    Challah Bread Recipe 94

13. The Remembering 95

    The Remembering Picture 102

14. The Book Goes to the Publisher 103

    Picture of Naomi and Ruth from Antique Shop 111

15. Praying for Israel 112

16. Pennies 119

    Sketch of the Unknown Child by Michael Swartz 126

17. Is it For Jews Only? 127

    Mr. Cohen's Asparagus Parmesan Recipe 134

18. Provoking to Jealousy 135

Conclusion 142
Other Books by the Author 147

Introduction

Some time back, I was asked to rewrite my first book (*Ruth 3,000 Years of Sleeping Prophecy Awakened*) in a format that our ten-year old granddaughter could read and understand. On numerous occasions, our little Rachel had asked to read Gramma's book, and this grandmother was not about to turn down a granddaughter's admirable request. Thus, I set out to tackle what I knew at the outset would be difficult. That book had taken ten years to write, and I would be attempting to reduce an in-depth Bible study to mere *Cliff Notes*. It was not long before I came to the sobering realization that to condense that work would greatly dilute many of the deep truths in Ruth, a sacrifice I was not willing to make.

Although I never again picked up that initial condensed version of Ruth, I also never laid it down in my mind. I wanted our little Rachel, and all of our grandchildren, armed with the truths in Ruth, but not at that great a price. However, there was something inside me clamoring to come to life, and so unrelenting were the pangs, that I soon realized it was my personal Jewish journey that must be written for our grandchildren. Although the Ruth book would have to wait until they were mentally and spiritually mature, there were incredible true stories bubbling up inside me that would not only astonish them, but would, I hoped, set each of them on their own pursuit of unconditional love for Israel and the Jewish people.

Writing these stories would also silence several admonishments I had received over the years from close friends who prodded me to make my Jewish experiences a matter of record lest the stories "go to the grave with me." I guess I never shared their same urgency, and besides, several were included in the Ruth book, so, for the most part, those friendly chastisements collected somewhere on the back burner of my then pressing agenda.

However, as I began to recollect, make outlines, place events in chronological order and write, I found myself possibly the most amazed of all. I had only considered these incidents as isolated events, never as part of a whole. I was astonished as an incredible story began to unfold. It was a journey where little by little God had allowed someone with no credentials, nil notoriety, "the least of these my brethren," into the deeper and deeper recesses of the world of Judaism. It was truly God doing what He does best: taking the least likely on a highly unlikely, God-sized journey.

Although there are many stories, I have chosen to include only those with a "wow factor," the ones that rocked my comfortable little world – the times where God used the off limits of Judaism to confound and mess up my perfectly good Christian rut. I wanted our grandchildren to see my intimate relationship with the enormous and incredibly personal God of the Universe, and I wanted them to crave this same relationship for themselves. However, the more I wrote, the more I longed for the Church to know these truths as well, and the extremes to which the God of Abraham, Isaac and Jacob will go to sanction unity between His Chosen and His Church.

It is incomprehensible to think that this has been a thirty-plus year journey, and I never saw the scope of it until now. Through it all, the one Absolute Constant has been God and God alone. This has been a walk of faith and I had to be open to the "rules" changing, if God so directed, which He did quite often. These were times when God challenged me with the little known Jewishness of Christianity, and with my willingness to embrace what God was vividly revealing: Jewish-Christian unity. He wanted the whole of my predictable life's canvas surrendered to His purpose, to alter at will, using His own ever-amazing, possibly unfamiliar, brush strokes. Was I willing to be His subject, or would I continue along in my status-quo Christianity?

I do not want to pass down my fathers' religion to my progeny or to anyone else for that matter. But, I do want to pass on an unsullied zeal for the Great God Jehovah that allows Him a canvas untouched by human hands, a canvas where He alone can be the Master Creator. This is the backdrop against which He can demonstrate His most creative work, and who knows but that one yielded life may be all He needs to usher Jewish-Christian relations into its finest hour – and yours may be that life.

Diane A. McNeil
diane@jewishgamechangers.com
Website: www.jewishgamechangers.com

1.

A Glimpse into God's Secret Place

"Game changer" is a 21st century slang term. At present it is not in standard dictionaries and is not a viable word for Scrabble. WordWeb Online defines game changer as a person who is a visionary, one who has new and different ideas that stand out from the crowd. The term is often used by the media when relating to sports, business, world conditions, etc. A game changer has the ability to instantly change the situation into something utterly different.

It has been more than thirty years since my first shocking game changer experience that, indeed, did instantly change my situation and forever alter my life's direction. In that briefest of moments, God lifted me out of my own agonizing circumstances and for a split second peeled back a divine layer that exposed something I never knew existed. I was allowed an intimate look into God's heart for Israel and the Jews and then left to respond in whatever manner I so chose. Would I revere God enough to lay aside my own personal pain and suffering and reach to embrace His, or would I continue to wallow in my own "no-hope-in-sight" existence? The stage was set for game changer number one.

I have replayed the incident hundreds of times in my mind – not lest I should forget, but because of the incredulity that the great God of all the ages would visit this inconsequential female and allow me a glimpse into His private chamber. After all these years, I still marvel that I was permitted into His place of anguish. I had been begging Him to come into mine and rescue me, never suspecting that He had his own such domain. Amazingly, yet so like God, this sudden encounter did more than merely forge a deeper, mutual bond between us; it forever altered my predictable, little religious world. I had never ventured beyond my comfortable Christian confines, and certainly would never have entertained breaching the unknowns of Judaism.

The year was 1975; the setting was a small, white, painted-brick home in suburban Memphis, Tennessee. On the outside looking in, it was the typical Christian-American family: a father, a mother and two blond headed, blue eyed little boys, ages eight and six. We were probably the epitome of the word average. My husband and I both worked outside the home struggling to make it from payday to payday, and, like most parents, we wanted the absolute best for our children. Although it was a financial strain, they were enrolled in a private Christian school that was housed at the little Baptist church where we were active Sunday mornings, Sunday nights and Wednesday nights. All was seemingly picture-perfect, with the exception of one not-so-minor glitch: Our oldest son was hyperactive.

Hyperactivity may seem to some a cop-out – a title to justify lack of discipline – but, if you have ever really lived it, you know it is all too real, and for the most part completely unresponsive to any form of control. It could and did unmask itself at the most inopportune times – school, home, church, parties, family gatherings, wherever and whenever. Hyperactivity has no boundaries. Sometimes we could identify what had gone awry, but for the most part, episodes came and went, and the elusive villain would win again. We tried everything known to us at the time: no TV, no bicycle, no friends, sitting in a corner, the peach tree switch, a belt, but, try as we did, we never seemed to corral that uninvited monster. I made our foods from scratch, eliminating all additives, artificial colors and flavorings; we used special toothpaste, soap and detergent, but nothing effectively altered this mysterious and uncharted course. We were for the most part left with, "Just deal with it." It was at the height of this intensely trying ordeal that God sent His first game changer.

On that particular night, as the boys were preparing for bed, our youngest decided to mimic his Dad's typical morning routine by styling his hair the same way, and then plastering it down with his Dad's hair spray. We thought, "How cute – trying to be like Daddy," never suspecting the tormenting toxins lurking in the fumes of that spray. Both sons slept in bunk beds in the same room, and as the house was small and their room next to the den with the TV, we always closed their door after tucking them in. This night was as all other nights.

The next morning as I was in the kitchen making breakfast and packing lunches, their bedroom door opened. What happened next seemed to suck the life right out of me. As I peered across the den toward their bedroom, our oldest son made his morning appearance. A nightmare unfolded. He crawled from their room on his elbows and belly like a soldier in the trenches, and dragged himself in that posture the entire length of the den into the kitchen. When he reached my feet, he looked up and screamed, "Good Morning, Mom!" I was dumbfounded! What could possibly have gone so tragically wrong in the nine hours while they slept? What sent him reeling?

My thoughts immediately raced to the dreaded call from school. They would grill us, for the hundredth time, as to why we could not control our son. After that would come the humiliating parent-teacher conference, which always ended condescendingly with, "And, are you having any marital problems?" That one infuriated me! How could the situation have gotten so out of hand? What did *we* do wrong? And, what on earth were we dealing with?

I tried with everything in me to maintain calm and rein my son in, knowing this was going to be a horrible day for everyone – parents, teachers, classmates and carpool riders. I continued the usual morning routine and got them off, then, immediately dropped to my knees in front of the couch and began pleading with the Lord in absolute desperation. I had done everything humanly possible; there was nothing else left in me. I could say that I had given it my very best, yet my best was not good enough.

I cried out in anguish, "Lord, I have done all I can do; if you do not help, then there is no help." In that instant the Lord spoke to me, and said, *"Now, do you see how I feel with my Israel?"* It was as if an electrifying charge had bolted through every fiber of my being. Nothing like this had ever happened to me. I moved from my kneeling position to sitting on the floor with my back against the couch, and thought, "What just happened?" Then, I replayed the words I had prayed and the Lord's reply, and it was one of those "Oh my goodness" moments.

In Exodus 4:22, God calls Israel His firstborn son. This eight-year old was our firstborn son. Scripture also tells us that some family members loathe Israel (consider the enemy nations surrounding Israel, most of whom are blood related), and the same was true with our son and some of our family members. I recall once a member of our family telling me (when no one else was in the room) that what I needed to do with this son was the same thing you do to a stubborn donkey – "knock him up beside the head with a two-by-four." He was not making a joke either; he meant every word. The ultimate irony in all of this is that many of the fiercest critics and enemies of Israel and the Jews have been so-called Christians. Sad to say, Ken and I experienced some of that with our son. Once, while at their Christian school, I passed one of the school administrators in the hall, who nonchalantly addressed me and said something very mean-spirited about our son, and then kept walking down the hall. There were only a few who loved him unconditionally. Our firstborn son was my heartbeat. It was not possible to love him any more than I did, and I knew the Lord must surely love His own firstborn indescribably more.

I am not perfect by any stretch, but with every resource known to me at the time, I had genuinely tried to control our son. In contrast, God is perfect, and His parenting skills (His Holy Word) are equally perfect. How dare any of us raise a hand against His firstborn, whether family, so-called Christian or outsider! God does not need us to discipline or judge His Israel and the Jewish people, but He will graciously welcome any and all genuine expressions of unconditional love.

After pondering the many ramifications of that life altering Jewish game changer, I sympathized with the Lord over His plight and said that I understood what He was saying to me (as much as is humanly possible). In that moment, I committed to pray for Israel every day for the rest of my life. I knew the absolute torment our situation was for us and knew that God was allowing it so that I could understand the Father's heart for His firstborn, Israel. Have I been one hundred percent faithful to my commitment? No, but there have been very few missed days. The amazing result has been that I have fallen in love with Israel and the Jews – unconditionally. I love her and them with everything in me, and God knows that right well.

And thou shalt say unto Pharaoh, Thus saith the Lord, Israel is my son, even my firstborn; and I say unto thee, Let my son go, that he may serve me: and if thou refuse to let him go, behold, I will slay thy son, even thy firstborn. Exodus 4:22-23

Prayer: Father, truly, your ways are not our ways – they are much, much higher. I tenderly thank you for that day and for your intimate intrusion into my little world. Thank you for opening your heart to me and for showing me what genuinely grieves and pains you. Lord God Almighty, please forgive me for the times I may have told degrading Jewish jokes, or used Jewish slurs. Oh God, please have mercy and let all these sins be as far from you as the East is from the West. Bless Israel, Lord, and I yield every part of my being for your use in loving her, esteeming her a million times more than self. I offer this prayer in the gentle and priceless Name of Jesus, Amen.

2.

My Ruth Encounter

S ome twenty years passed between God's first Jewish game changer, when He allowed me entrance into His secret chamber of heartache, and my second surprise visitation.

My Ruth Encounter occurred on a Sunday morning, August 19, 1995, and it happened just as suddenly and as unexpectedly as the first. I was at home alone, sick in bed with a debilitating case of tonsillitis. Ken had gone to church, along with the only one of our three sons still living at home. I lay there with fever and the frightening sensation of my throat closing up. I was so miserable that I genuinely felt like dying; I remember praying for the Lord to go ahead and take me because Heaven sounded much better than what I was experiencing. I meant it. As I was selfishly praying and having my final rites pity party, suddenly a voice, as clearly as any I had ever heard audibly, spoke in my spirit and said, "Hi, my name is Ruth, and I'm meditative grocery stores." I did not know which was more jolting, the experience or the baffling words. In astonishment I mulled, "Where did that come from?" Instantly I lost all sense of my own pitiful condition, and leapt from the bed and went over to my desk for paper and a pencil with which to write down the perplexing words. (I have learned over the years to record the Lord's words instantly when He speaks. Each word is critical and may dissipate just as quickly as it came.) My Bible was on the desk, so I grabbed it and crawled back into bed. I knew intuitively that this experience concerned the Book of Ruth, so I anxiously turned to her pages anticipating something God-sized!

I read through the entire book (four chapters), and, much to my dismay, found absolutely nothing different from all other times I had read Ruth. Yet, I knew with all the certainty of Heaven that God Almighty had spoken to me, and I declared that I was not letting go until I understood the meaning of that divine encounter.

Over the next few weeks and months, I pored over Ruth in every translation I could get my hands on and always with the same result – absolutely nothing that would warrant such an intrusion. I combed through Bible studies, commentaries and Bible dictionaries – still nothing. I knew without a doubt that I had heard from the Lord but also felt I had just about exhausted all available resources. I decided to step back and take a fresh approach. I understood I was to be meditating on the Book of Ruth; that part was unmistakable, but I had no idea what was meant by the grocery stores part.

On a whim, I decided to phone my local grocery to see if I might uncover any clues. At the time, we lived in an upscale community on the outskirts of Memphis, Tennessee and had a large, newly renovated and very well stocked grocery. I dialed their number, and when the lady on the other end answered, I explained to her that I was doing a little study, and asked if she could tell me how many items they stock on their store shelves. To my astonishment, she spouted off the answer without the slightest hesitation, "Thirty thousand normally and up to 50,000 for major holidays." I was shocked, not only with her ready answer, but with the unbelievable volume of items contained on my store's shelves.

I thanked her, hung up the phone and hastily went to my own kitchen shelves to take inventory. I calculated, "If I have 500 items, then I have 1.67 per cent of the 30,000 available. And, if I have 1,500 (which sounded like a lot), then that is still only a mere five per cent." I concluded, "Wow, percentage-wise, I have very little of what is available to me." At that moment, I realized what the Lord was trying to show me. I rarely venture beyond the norm in my routine grocery shopping – same meals, same aisles, same ingredients. That very thing was true of my approach to the Book of Ruth. He was showing me that I knew very little of the truths concealed in Ruth's pages because I was approaching her in the same manner as I did my grocery shopping. Those buried treasures were available, for sure, but only if I dared to venture beyond my norm; I had to make the change. I had to shop unfamiliar shelves, select items totally foreign to me, bring them into my own life and hands-on experience them. The goods were there for the taking, but only if I dared to alter my shopping habits. It was all up to me. I was the one who had to move. How badly did I want to see into the deep recesses of

Ruth? Was I willing to put myself out there and trust the Lord completely? Could I, by faith, trust His unknown path that might possibly be uncomfortable or take me places I would rather not go? The only response God desired from me was, "Here am I Lord, send me – nothing held back."

I recall one vacation when Ken and I had taken a day trip across the border to a tourist town in Mexico. I was shocked at how quickly the landscape changed, but genuinely eager to have this new experience. We shopped a little, looking for those bargains I had heard about, and then stumbled upon a local grocery. As I am all about kitchens and cooking, I had to go inside and take a quick peek. I soon discovered that if it were not for the pictures on the containers, I would have a very hard time knowing what to buy or how to put a meal together (and, even then, many of the pictures were of things I did not recognize).

On another occasion while vacationing in Colorado, we went to a local grocery to stock up for our week's stay. I had made out menus for our meals and had prepared a shopping list. It never occurred to me that what was everyday fare in the South was not to be had in other parts of the United States. What was this Southern girl to do without her cornbread and black-eyed peas?

The Lord spoke "meditative grocery stores" (plural) to me and provided those experiences so I would grasp that spiritually Ruth far exceeds the mere contrast between my kitchen shelves and my suburban grocery store's shelves. He wanted me out of my small self-confinement. There is an enormous spiritual storehouse waiting out there, but its vastness cannot be accessed by continuing to do the same things in the same way. He had my attention. I did not want Ruth as usual, and I was willing to go beyond myself into whatever situations necessary so He could reveal those hidden treasures.

As my journey progressed, I was overwhelmed to find that God literally used the words spoken to me by the lady at my grocery: "Thirty thousand normally and up to 50,000 for major holidays." That was no coincidence. I was amazed when I discovered that there are three major Jewish Holidays the Hebrew children are commanded to observe in Jerusalem. These three are alluded to in the Book of Ruth, though not specifically mentioned. When these three major holidays are brought into play, it is as if the prophetic understanding of Ruth nearly doubles – just as the items on my own grocery shelves nearly double for our major holidays.

I will be the first to admit that what was spoken to me in my Ruth encounter in 1995 was beyond strange. But, God's ways are not our ways; His thoughts are not our thoughts. Are we willing to get out of our predictable, confined Christian boxes and step out into a world of faith, not knowing where the next step may take, but knowing and believing in the One who is the Author and Finisher of our faith? How dull our existence would be without the exhilarating unknowns of the walk of faith!

I did go on that Ruth journey – a ten-year adventure that I would not trade for anything. Did God get me out of my comfort zone during that time? The answer lies in the many succeeding Jewish game changers. Gaining that understanding of Ruth took me to Israel with Messianic Jews, afforded me Hebrew classes with an Israeli Jew, carried me to Jewish weddings, funerals, bar and bat mitzvahs, circumcision ceremonies, Shabbat dinners, had me intertwining my life with Holocaust survivors, found me working with the Memphis Jewish Federation – and that may not be the half of it. I had to go where I had never gone before, never entertained the idea of going before, for the sake of understanding what God so genuinely and so lovingly wanted to show me.

He loves us – all of us – and eagerly desires to have a close, personal relationship with each of us, but it must be on His terms and not on ours. How sad that most Christians go through this life setting their own parameters. They would never do this or never do that. But, parallel that rigidity with our Lord's walk. Most of us would never stoop so low as to dine with a cheat, a liar and a thief, or ask an openly blatant whore for a drink of water. We are far too religious for that. Shame on us! I wonder what would happen if God's children laid all pre-conceived religious notions at the foot of the cross, and said, "Here am I, Lord, send me, and I am not going to tell you how or where; I am simply going to willingly obey." If our Christianity is stagnant, perhaps it is because we have come to an impasse somewhere and stopped listening.

There is yet another, uncomfortable side to all of this that must be addressed at the very outset. We not only have to be willing to go wherever and whenever, but it is also imperative that we set our spiritual houses in order before the journey. That part alone keeps most from ever taking that first step on the walk of faith. Have I honored my father and my mother? If not, then it must be made right, and if they are gone, then we must earnestly confess it to God and ask His forgiveness. Is there a sibling or work associate or neighbor with whom we have unresolved issues? He will not launch us out into the deeps until all is resolved. It may be extremely hard, but I can promise you that it will be well worth any momentary humiliation.

I remember one occasion early in my journey when I was feeling absolutely confident that all was right in my life. I was out for my morning walk, praising God, blessing Him and just loving all over Him, basking in the moment. Then I said to Him, "Lord, I want you to show me anything, and I mean anything at all that I have done or not done that needs to be made right, and I will do it." As soon as those words came out of my mouth, I saw in my mind my kitchen silverware drawer and a certain set of steak knives. My heart sank, and I thought, "Oh, no, Lord, not that – anything but that."

Years before, my 18-year old first cousin had been killed in a car wreck. Her mother (my mother's sister) called to ask Ken if he would go to the towed-car lot and collect all of her daughter's personal belongings from her car. He did so and then brought the things to our house for me to take to my aunt after the funeral. Under the seat of the car, Ken found several new steak knives still in their individual wrappers. These were free with fill-ups at a local gas station. I knew she was probably collecting them for her hope chest, because I knew she was seriously dating a young man that my aunt did not like. I thought I would save my aunt from additional hurt, so I held them back, never intending to use them. Yet, over the years they somehow found their way into my silverware drawer. Those were the steak knives the Lord showed me.

The thought of calling my aunt made me sick all over, not just because I had done something so incredibly stupid, but because she was a bitter, angry, contentious woman whose whole existence seemed one disaster after another. Part of me considered ignoring God's prodding, but the other part knew that if I really meant what I had prayed, then I had no option but to call and confess my sin to her. I prayed hard for favor and dialed her number. I told her what I had done and my rationale for doing it. She was so gracious – much more gracious than I deserved. Her response was, "Diane, I can't think of anyone I would rather have those steak knives than you." This undeserved kindness brings tears to my eyes even now. God is so good, and He will never leave us or forsake us. He just wants us without baggage, and rightfully so.

How much of ourselves are we willing to give him? And, what are our terms of service? Oh, friend, He gave us His best, His all; let us not give Him anything less! May it be with us as was penned by the hymnist, "Nothing between my soul and the Savior."

> *And Ruth said, Intreat me not to leave thee, or to return from following after thee: for whither thou goest, I will go; and where thou lodgest, I will lodge: thy people shall be my people, and thy God my God: Where thou diest, will I die, and there will I be buried: the Lord do so to me, and more also, if ought but death part thee and me.* Ruth 1:16-17.

Prayer: Oh, Father, where would any of us be without your long-suffering grace? Oh, Lord, please forgive us for the times we have grossly frustrated that grace. May we, like Ruth, turn our backs on our former, pagan life of self-service, and may we set out on the path of going where you go, lodging where you lodge, making your people our people, making you our one and only God, and dying and being laid to rest in this unmovable position – all for our good and your glory! Lord, bottom line, we love you and know that without you, life would have no meaning or purpose. May your Name be eternally praised! In the powerful Name of Jesus I pray, Amen.

3.

A Birthday Surprise

I was so content with the arrangement I had with the Lord in that first Jewish game changer – that of praying for Israel every day for the rest of my life. I liked being behind the scenes. It was such a safe, comfortable place, and I had to exert very little effort in my calling. However, my status-quo little Christian landscape was about to undergo a dramatic change of scenery.

One day as I was out running errands, I decided to tune in to a local Christian radio station. I rarely listen to the radio or music; I prefer silence. But, for whatever reason, I wanted the radio on that particular day. Soon I was listening to an announcement that a local Messianic Jewish Synagogue (Jewish believers in Jesus) was hosting an area-wide Passover Seder and the public was invited. As if that were not intriguing enough, the announcer said that the event was being held on April tenth – my birthday. My heart began racing. I intuitively knew this was meant for me; it was my birthday present! Everything inside me became alive with mysterious excitement. And, even though I knew God was the Orchestrator, I could not help but feel a slight tinge of apprehension, wondering what He was up to.

A couple of days later Ken asked me, "Honey, your birthday is coming up. What would you like to do?" I did not hesitate. "I want to go to a Passover Seder" (I knew what Passover meant, but I did not have a clue what a Seder was.) Shock registered on his face. I told him what had happened in the car, and he said, "Well, if that's what you really want to do, get the tickets and we'll go." I love that man!

I looked up the synagogue in the phone book and jotted down the address, then headed over to buy the tickets. They were located in a very nice part of Memphis in a converted bungalow-style house. As I entered the building, I was keenly aware that I did not know these people. This might even be some sort of cult. Did I really know what I was getting myself into? I rambled my way through a couple of rooms and up some steps before locating the receptionist. I introduced myself, and she did the same. Her name was Doris, and she was Jewish. Doris was a little older than I, with a comfortable grandmotherly demeanor. She was warm and inviting and had me captivated almost instantly. But, I was on guard and determined not to be taken in by her possible craftiness – just in case.

I told Doris what I wanted. She appeared thrilled (I could not understand that), and acted like she really wanted us to come, which made me even more wary. I am a no frills, stick-to-business type person, and this kind of instant, seemingly genuine "friendship" made me uneasy. So, with all of my spiritual "maturity," I decided to test the spirits and see if their agenda was of God.

By this time she and I had moved from her office into a small gift shop. She was retrieving the two tickets from a little money box in which she had deposited my check. I craftily asked, "Tell me, do you think Jesus is coming soon?" Without the slightest hesitation, she turned to the small window behind her and pulled back the simple white muslin curtain, and peered up into the sky with a longing like none I have ever seen before or since. "I look for Him every morning," she said. I was stunned. Even I do not look for Him like that. Leaving the synagogue, I was humbled and ashamed. What right had I to judge these people? She had silenced this skeptic and became another of my growing Jewish game changers.

The day of the event arrived and Ken and I were both understandably apprehensive. This was a Jewish thing. What were we doing going to a Jewish thing? Would we stick out like sore thumbs? Would it be obvious to everyone there that we were not Jewish? Who would we sit with – would Jews really want to sit with Gentiles? What were we supposed to do, and how were we supposed to act; and what is a Seder anyway?

The synagogue had rented a large banquet hall for the evening. At the door, we were welcomed by greeters from the congregation eager to assist. I noticed a long table in the foyer displaying Judaica (Jewish) books and items for sale and made a mental note to browse through these before leaving. We were escorted into the banquet hall and began looking around for available seating. We spotted an out-of-the-way table and asked the people seated there if we could join them. We were pleasantly surprised to find ourselves sitting with other first-timers who also were not Jewish. One of them was a Baptist pastor from Missouri who, during the week, attended a local seminary where Ken just happened to be on one of the committees, so we began to breathe a great deal easier.

The facility was festively decorated. I spied a band (for real?) and a dance floor (shock to my Baptist system!). People were excitedly milling around, apparently greatly anticipating the evening. Of course, Ken and I did not do the milling, but we did do some serious spectating. Every once in a while I would catch him giving me that look that says, "What on earth have you gotten us into this time?"

I took inventory of our table setting; it was definitely different. There were bowls of water, piles of parsley, a bone, some red stuff, something that looked like horseradish (surely not), a plate of that bread that Jews eat at Passover called matzo and a hard-boiled egg. These tickets had been somewhat pricey, and I could sense my husband, who is passionate about mealtime, sizing up the situation and wondering if there was going to be any real food. (I was too.)

The Rabbi stepped to the podium and asked everyone to take their seats because the celebration was about to begin. We found out that each of these strange items on our table was used to tell the story of that first Passover when the Hebrew children left Egypt in haste. We learned that Seder means "order" – the telling of the order of the events of the Exodus from Egypt. The parsley represented their meager diet while in slavery. The bone depicted the Passover lamb. The horseradish symbolized their bitter, tearful suffering. The red "stuff," charoset, was a mixture of chopped apples, nuts, cinnamon and wine, reminiscent of the mortar used by the Hebrew children in building the palaces and pyramids of Egypt. The matzo represented the bread of affliction. And, the boiled egg symbolized the Temple that is no longer standing in Jerusalem.

What Ken and I found so fascinating was how they purposefully connected each of these items to the ultimate Passover Lamb, our slavery to sin, and the sacrificial blood setting captives free. Over and over they praised Jesus – Yeshua as they call Him in Hebrew – which means salvation. It was so reassuring to discover that their beliefs about Jesus are exactly the same as ours.

What a "forever" evening that was – one I will always cherish! There was singing and dancing, a children's drama, adults and youngsters dancing by themselves and together, "hide and seek" and so much more. As I watched the dancers, I conjured up mental pictures of King David dancing before the Lord. The same Jewish blood that pulsed through his veins was now running through these dancers' veins. There was such gaiety at this celebration. I felt certain that they danced with every bit of exuberance as did their ancestral King David. These people were not conscious of themselves or anyone else in the room; they were only conscious that they were whole-heartedly worshiping a Holy God, their Deliverer, who is worthy of extravagant worship and praise. (Oh, and there was a full meal at the end – no disappointments anywhere.)

My favorite moment came at the very end, just before we were dismissed. We knew the event was coming to a close. The Passover story had been told, our stomachs were fully content and it was getting late. But I noticed several men begin to stir. I watched as each removed his shoes and socks and rolled up his pants legs. Then, each man took a prayer shawl (the rectangular garment with the tassels on the four corners, also known as a tallit) and walked to the dance floor. Soulful, stirring music began to play. They took their prayer shawls and completely covered their heads and then drew into a tight circle, shoulders touching and heads bowed. They began to dance, never lifting their heads and never removing their head coverings. A reverential hush settled over the entire hall. There was no movement or sound of any kind except for the stirring music and the muffled, rhythmic thud of bare feet striking against the hardwood floor. It was obvious that each of us felt we had entrance into a holy place and that to speak or move would disturb the divine communion between these worshipers and the God of Abraham, Isaac and Jacob. I felt tears welling up in my eyes, and glanced over at Ken to discover his eyes had welled up, too. Rarely have I had such an intense spiritual experience. When the music and the dancing ceased, the hush lingered on; it was a moment we wanted to preserve for as long as possible. Truly, we had witnessed man communing with God.

I had never before entertained any thoughts of Christianity connecting with Judaism, but that was exactly what happened that evening. God, through one of His little Jewish game changers, had disturbed my perfectly good Christian world. I loved being with these people. I loved learning these Jewish things. It was definitely the unknown, but it was an unknown that was powerfully wooing me. I wanted more, and God knew it.

Sadly, the evening came to a close, and once again we settled back into our rushed, harried, workaday worlds. I continued my daily prayers for Israel, wondering if perchance God had yet more Jewish game changers on the horizon.

> *Rejoice ye <u>with</u> Jerusalem, and be glad <u>with</u> her, all ye that love her: rejoice for joy <u>with</u> her . . . . Isaiah 66:10.*

Prayer: Oh, Father, thank you for your rich surprises, which take us out of ourselves and position us in strategic places. We love your invitations and being about our Father's business. Please see through to completion this good work you have begun in us, and gently correct us if we dare to put up a finger to stop your processes. Father, we want no part of hindrance to your Kingdom, but we do want all inclusion in promoting your will. We love you with an everlasting love, because you make such an incredible thing possible. With grateful hearts we bless you and thank you in the Name that is above every name, Amen.

4.

Ask and Ye Shall Receive

Q uite some time passed after that delightful Messianic Passover Seder and my next game changer. The Seder was one of the most exciting evenings of my life, but time moves on, and so did we.

I was continuing to pray for Israel daily, as promised in that first game changer. Our oldest son, the hyper one, was now grown, through college and had moved away to pursue his career. And, although the crisis of hyperactivity was no longer an issue, nothing would ever alter my vow; it was a commitment for life.

I often get up in the middle of the night to pray. I awaken suddenly and know it is my call to prayer. I have tried to stay in bed all warm and snuggly and pray, but that just does not work. I have to get myself out of bed. If I roll over and ignore the prompting, there is such a miserable prick in my Spirit all the next day. But I do not want you to think that I am some sort of powerhouse prayer warrior who prays through the night. There are many nights that I fall asleep on my knees, or while sitting on the floor, or my mind wanders to personal, pressing matters that try and rob Israel of her time. It is an ongoing battle to be faithful to: "Lord, every day for the rest of my life . . ."

One night as I was up praying for Israel, I was again shocked by another of those surprise visitations. As I was praying, I distinctly heard the Lord say "B'rit Hadasha" (Hebrew for New Covenant), the name of the Messianic Jewish Synagogue that had hosted the Passover Seder to which Ken and I had gone. I thought, "Wow! That is strange. I guess the Lord wants me to pray for them, too." I prayed something probably very simple and thought nothing more about it. I finished my prayers and went back to bed.

Mid-morning the next day, Ken phoned from work to ask if I could meet him for lunch to sign some papers he needed. I certainly did not mind signing papers if it meant a free lunch. So, at the agreed-upon time and place, he and I met. We drove up at the same time, so we actually walked into the restaurant together. As we entered through the first set of glass double doors, I glanced up and saw through the glass entry the Rabbi from B'rit Hadasha, the synagogue that had hosted the Passover Seder. I quickly grabbed Ken's arm and said, "I have to tell you something. When I was up praying last night, the Lord said 'B'rit Hadasha' to me, and there is that Rabbi!" He looked at me like I had lost my mind, and I thought, "Okay, don't say I didn't warn you."

We passed through the second set of glass doors and were soon escorted to our table. We placed our orders and were directed to the salad bar. This particular dining chain is noted for its long salad bar that typically runs through the middle of the restaurant. We approached the line, and my precious, adorable, Southern gentleman husband went first. I followed behind, ever-conscious of the Rabbi's presence. Suddenly, the Rabbi left his table and walked over to the salad bar – right behind me. I thought, "Oh no, this is God's doing and I have no choice, I have to say something." I knew the Lord had instigated the whole thing, but, nonetheless, a myriad of thoughts raced through my head: Are Gentiles actually permitted to speak to Rabbis? And, what if that Gentile is a woman? Will I be committing the unpardonable? Fearful or not, I dared not miss out on anything the Lord had in store. I turned to the Rabbi and said, "You're the rabbi from B'rit Hadasha, aren't you?" He replied affirmatively. I introduced Ken and myself and told him that we had been to one of their Passover Seders, and what a blessing it had been. I then cowardly said that the Lord had impressed me the night before to pray for their synagogue. I was not about to tell him that the Lord had spoken to me because I was sure they would bring out the guys in the white jackets and whisk me away. He graciously thanked me for my prayers, and under my breath I said, "Okay, Lord, I did what I was supposed to do, and now I'm out of here." Hurriedly, I finished making my salad and took my leave.

I was seated with my back to the salad bar so I could no longer see the Rabbi or Ken, who was lingering over the dressings and toppings. I waited for him to come for what seemed an inordinate amount of time, yet he did not return even though he was in line ahead of me. I stole a quick glance over my shoulder, and to my absolute shock I saw Ken and the Rabbi engrossed in conversation. The longer I waited, the harder my heart pounded in my chest. Finally, Ken appeared, and before sitting down, looked at me and said, "Guess what?" Holding my breath I said, "What?" He said, "We are going to Israel with them in June." An array of emotions raced through every part of me. I was ecstatic; I was thrilled; I was beside myself; yet, there was also something intensely guarded in me. Why would Jews invite Gentiles to come with them to their Promised Land? Did they not believe we were unclean, lesser than they? I do not know why I had such deep feelings of inferiority, but they were forefront and they were genuine.

(I must interject something here that still overwhelms me. About two weeks prior to this Jewish game changer luncheon, I was riding along in my car talking to the Lord, and in that conversation I reminded Him that He knew I had always wanted to go to Israel but He also knew I felt unworthy to as much as set one foot in His Holy Land. However, I also knew that Scripture says we have not because we ask not, so, based on that authority, I was asking Him for a trip to Israel. He could do with it whatever He wanted, but I was asking. That was my prayer – just that simple.)

As time drew near for our divinely appointed trip, we began receiving invitations to Shabbat (another word for Sabbath) dinners in the homes of some of the Jewish people who were also going on the trip. We learned so much; it was as though in their presence there was constant, unconscious teaching. These special times were inexpressible blessings, and we had not even boarded the plane.

The greatly anticipated event finally arrived, and it was everything I had ever dreamed and much, much more. I cannot relate every aspect, but will share just a couple of incidents. The first came our first night there, which was spent in a kibbutz in Tiberias. We arrived after dark, so we had no idea of our surroundings. The next morning Ken and I were not awakened by the sun streaming through the window, or birds singing or a curiosity to scope the landscape, but rather, we awoke with the Messianic Jewish man in the unit next to ours outside playing his guitar and singing to the Lord – in his Promised Land. He was worshipping with songs of praise (some in Hebrew) to the God of his fathers in his own homeland. Ken and I lay there basking in the words, the music and the overflowing Jewish heart. We dared not speak or make a sound lest we disturb the sanctity between him and God. We were privy to a Jewish believer worshipping Messiah Yeshua from the very depths of his being. What an incredible beginning!

The other event that is eternally etched in my mind occurred the day we went to the River Jordan.

But first, I must digress and go back many years prior so you can understand the impact of that particular experience. When I was eight years old, we were having a revival in our little Baptist church in Lambert, Mississippi, where I was born and raised. I remember the church being full and my sitting in the balcony, which we kids rarely did because our parents did not usually allow it. When the invitation to give your life to Christ was given, I peeped to see what was happening down below, and spied my two older sisters going forward. One was two years older than I, and the other, three. When I saw them going forward to be saved, I immediately thought, "Well, I'm not going to be left out", so I "got saved," too. I think it is fair to say that was not my true salvation experience.

Then, when I was about twelve years old, we had a youth revival and almost all the youth went forward. Again, I was not going to be left out. I have no recollection of confessing my sins or asking Jesus to come into my heart and save me, and there was no counseling on either occasion. Sadly, what I do recall is being handed a clipboard and being asked to fill out the pertinent information and that was all I had to do to "be saved." I continued to be active in church and to read my Bible every day, but I sincerely could not tell you my true spiritual condition. After Ken and I married and moved to Memphis, we joined a strong, dynamic, Bible-believing church, and although I felt that somewhere I had been saved, I could not put my finger on a time or a place, so there was always a nagging uncertainty.

I remember often going to revivals and the preacher saying that if you did not have your baptism on the right side of your salvation that you really needed to get it in order. I would fervently pray for the Lord to reveal to me what I should do. I had no idea when I was saved, so He was going to have to be the one to show me if I needed to be baptized again. I told Him I did not mind that it might be embarrassing; that really did not bother me. I just wanted it to be Him calling the shots. I had called far too many on my own, and I did not want that ever again.

Fast-forward to Israel and our little group visiting the Jordan River. Without my having any pre-conceived notion of what was going on, the Rabbi stepped into the Jordan River and asked if anyone wanted him to baptize them. Instantly, I knew this was my time! Every emotion in me was suddenly alive with excitement; this was what I had been waiting for and praying about for years. This was my time to be baptized – my real baptism – and God Himself had ordained that it be performed by a Jewish Rabbi in the same river where His Son was baptized. It was as though God was inextricably weaving me into His Jewish people – mystery of mysteries – a Mississippi-born, Southern-raised woman with no note-worthy credentials intertwined with His Chosen People! What a truly miraculous, God-sized Jewish game changer! With each of these unexpected, unsolicited, life-changing phenomena, my heart embraced more and more the Chosen Seed of Israel. I had truly fallen in love with His people – a never-ending love affair.

(One more thing about the baptism: as I was hurrying to get into the water, there was someone a little faster than I – my precious husband. The Rabbi actually baptized him first, and then me, and I have to tell you, "I love God's order.")

There were so many wonderful experiences on that trip, and I can truthfully say that not at any time did Ken or I ever feel like second-rate citizens or step-children. Instead, I would have to say that they esteemed us over themselves. I may have felt inferior, but never, ever did they display any attitude of superiority.

As we boarded the plane for the return flight home, we looked at each other with that deep longing inside and said, "I'm not ready to leave." We had such an odd sense of belonging and wondered if God really meant for Jew and Gentile to be so intimately connected.

Behold, how good and how pleasant it is for brethren to dwell together in unity! Psalm 133:1.

Prayer: Father, a thousand lifetimes would not be enough to say "thank you." You are such a benevolent, loving, sensitive Father;

oh, how truly blessed we are to be called the children of the Most High God! Thank you for your divine appointments, and thank you that you also love for your Gentile children to walk those sacred streets in Jerusalem and see the land that is the choicest in all the world. It is an amazing place, Lord, and we delight with you in your choosing. All praise and honor be unto you, world without end! In the sweet Name of Jesus, Amen.

5.

The Lone Gentile in Hebrew Class

We loved our time in Israel with Messianic Jews, but sadly, our Holy Land experience had its ending. We both yearn for a return trip to the Promised Land, but have been spoiled by our first one and want only that tour where God is once again our Travel Agent and Orchestrator of the entire affair.

We arrived home and reluctantly slipped back into our old routines, but my heart ached to cling to that Jewish connection. When our schedules permitted, we attended Shabbat services on Saturday mornings at the little Messianic synagogue, humbly grateful for each opportunity to further meld our lives with theirs. It was on one such Saturday morning that God presented my next Jewish game changer.

Ken and I entered the synagogue and were handed the weekly bulletins. The services had not yet begun, so we had a few minutes to read through our handouts. To my astonishment, I spied a notice that the Jewish Community Center was offering Hebrew classes for beginners on Tuesday evenings at seven, and the price was $20. Everything inside me began jumping up and down. I had wanted to take Hebrew for as long as I could remember. It was a personal frustration for me when a preacher would define a term in Hebrew and I would have to take his word for it. I wanted to be able to read the original text for myself. And, as quirky as this may sound, I also wanted to pronounce correctly all those Hebrew names listed in the Bible. I could only imagine how badly I was mutilating some person's name (and I was).

Tuesday evenings were perfect; we had nothing on our schedules for that night of the week. I make it a practice not to leave Ken on week nights because he works so hard and so long, and I do not want to take away from the little time we have together. However, I felt strongly that this class qualified as an exception to the rule.

But, I had to know that attending the class was God's will. I did not want to be outside of His choosing, and I especially did not want to be in a Jewish arena without God's say-so. I silently prayed, "Lord, you know I have always wanted to take Hebrew, but I want to know that this is your will. So, Lord, if this is your doing, then please let Ken see this and be the one to suggest it." That prayer was still on my lips when Ken leaned over and pointed to the announcement in the bulletin and said, "You've always wanted to take Hebrew; you ought to do this." I can assure you he did not have to say it twice. "Hebrew 101, here I come!"

I phoned the Jewish Community Center the following Monday and made the arrangements, and on Tuesday night headed out to my first-ever Hebrew class. Even though I knew with all certainty it was God's design, fear and excitement raced through me. This was uncharted territory. I remember praying as I was driving to that first class, and every subsequent class thereafter, "Lord, set a guard at my lips; don't let me say anything I shouldn't, but let me say everything I should."

I arrived at the Jewish Community Center a little ahead of schedule and asked at the front desk for the location of the class, then went to the designated room. Oh, the thoughts running through my head about what these people might say about me: What on earth is that Gentile doing in *our* class? Let's turn up our noses at her. Let's shun her and maybe she'll go away. Would they embarrass me? Would I embarrass myself? I was petrified! I sat as far back in the room as was possible, and would have sat outside the door if I could have gotten away with it. I glanced around the classroom at the individual faces, trying to assess how out-of-place I might be. I could not know for certain, but it appeared to me that I might be the only Gentile in the entire group. There were about a dozen females, all of whom seemed to know each other, and one lone male. (Later, I learned that he and I were the only Gentiles. He was a local pastor who only came to a couple of classes before dropping out. He was probably intimidated by all the women.)

The teacher took her place at the front of the room and began to address the group. Struck by her heavy, foreign accent, I knew that these Southern ears better listen intently or my time here might meet an even swifter demise. She introduced herself: "My name is

Naomi." I nearly fell out of my chair. It was only a short while back that God had spoken to me about the Book of Ruth (whose main character is Naomi). As a matter of fact, I was in the very beginning stages of researching and writing the Ruth book (another reason for my strong desire to take this class). And, suddenly, standing before me, God had placed an Israeli Jew named Naomi? (She actually spells her name with an "e", but I am using the traditional Biblical spelling.) I learned that night that my instructor had been born and raised in Israel, was a lawyer by profession and that she and her family had only been living in America a few years. Amazing! A citizen of the State of Israel was about to teach Gentile, Mississippi-born-and-raised Diane, Hebrew! Is that not somewhat like in the book of Ruth (where an Israeli Jew – Naomi – teaches a Gentile – Ruth)? There was no doubt in my mind that this was a God assignment, and while there was anxiety for certain, there was also a sense of awe and wonder at being in this place, at this time and with these people. What a phenomenal Jewish game changer!

Over the next few weeks, the class dwindled to about seven ladies, and that is where it remained for several years as we all learned Hebrew and got to know each other. Meanwhile, Naomi, and I became as close as sisters. Even now as I sit and write about her, my heart instantly overflows with love, warmth and a sincere appreciation for all she has meant to me and all I have gleaned from her on this incredible journey. Naomi and I talked most every day, and I was at her house most weeks. At the time, she still had teenagers at home, while Ken's and mine were grown. I watched her intense Jewish mothering, how seriously she took her children's education, her selflessness when it came to her children, and her genuine love for and appreciation of her husband. It was as if I were in a one-on-one classroom every minute I was with her, whether at our Hebrew class on Tuesday nights, in her home or on a long phone conversation. Every moment was for me a learning opportunity.

However, I was only seeing a small portion of the puzzle. I did feel at the time that my taking Hebrew was vital to my accurately interpreting and substantiating my writing on Ruth. But Naomi and all the ladies in that class were providing so much more. They were illustrating Jewish life before my ever-watchful eyes, not consciously, but simply by going about their normal, day-to-day routines. Often I would learn from them something that pertained to Ruth that would not register until much, much later. Neither they nor I could ever have imagined that my going to their children's weddings, their grandsons' circumcision ceremonies, their family funerals, and on and on, were all lessons in Ruth. They were going about their daily lives and I was being allowed private entrance into that incomparable domain. I could understand Ruth in no other way than to live it out through their Jewish lives.

I learned about Orthodox, Reformed, Conservative and Messianic Judaism, about keeping kosher, circumcisions, weddings, deaths, burials, adoptions, bar mitzvahs, bat mitzvahs, and on and on. Actually, I did not learn it; I lived it as they embraced me and took me on this incredible journey right alongside them. *Schlep* is a good Yiddish word (a dialect spoken by Jews in Europe). It means to carry something, such as schlepping in the groceries. Well, they schlepped me through all of these adventures with neither of us conscious of the much larger picture. God was unfolding the truths concealed in the pages of Ruth through these lovely lives in order that this Gentile might see and understand and write with authority. I was not getting a bird's-eye view; I had a front row, interactive seat.

I will never forget one day when Naomi told me she had something she wanted to ask me. She cautioned me that she was being quite serious, but wanted me to consider it carefully. She said that she trusted me completely and if anything were to happen to her and her husband before their children were grown, she wanted to know if Ken and I would consider raising them. I was stunned and honored. She said that the grandparents were old and that there were no aunts and uncles who could raise them. Of course, I told her we would, but let's back away and consider this for a moment.

Why would she trust me that much, to leave me her most treasured possession? Ken and I are not in the same financial bracket as they, so it was not for what we could provide financially. I am still asking myself why. The best answer I can come up with is because God gave me unconditional love for her and her family. I cringe at most people who speak of unconditional love, wondering if they were to be challenged in that area, what really might be exposed.

Unconditional love is looking past all exterior attributes, regardless of what is manifested, and loving the heart. It is not being swayed by what we see or hear, but by being heart-focused. Can we love someone unconditionally who uses words for which our mothers washed our mouths out with soap? Can we love someone unconditionally who has no place for our Redeemer? Can we love someone unconditionally who might be curt, forward and possibly rude? If you say you love someone unconditionally, then there can be no parameters – none whatsoever. I asked God to give me unconditional love for the Jewish people, and I pray that He has. And, you know who has benefitted? I have, without a doubt, and hopefully many Jews have as well from me, but the one that has most benefitted by this unconditional love is the Kingdom of God. It is not about us. He is worth it all, and that is why we do it.

Well, their children are now grown and established in highly professional, successful careers, so our raising them was never an issue, but more importantly, Naomi is still around, loving on me and I on her. She remains ever my cherished friend and my highly esteemed information highway into the world of Judaism.

I believe God wants laborers who are willing to walk out this journey – no matter the route, no matter how long it may take and no matter the difficulties incurred along the way. "Many are called but few are chosen." Our beloved pastor recently said that the better translation for this verse is, "Many are called but few choose to go." This is not for those who want instant gratification or who have underlying personal agendas, but it is for those who believe God's Word, who know that His covenant with Israel is everlasting and who want to be in on what God is doing with His Chosen and His Church in these last days.

> *Then saith he unto his disciples, The harvest truly is plenteous, but the labourers are few; pray ye therefore the Lord of the harvest, that he will send forth labourers into his harvest.* Matthew 9:37-38

Prayer: Father, thank you for hearing my heart's cry to learn Hebrew, but I know now that you put that deep longing in me from the very beginning. You did not satisfy my longing; you satisfied your longing that you placed in me. I love your language, Lord, and love praying scriptural passages back to you in their original tongue. What an incredible privilege. Father, I thank you that you are equally so personalized and individualized with all of your children. Your love and provisions are vast beyond measure. "What is man that thou art mindful of him," but you are! You are beyond amazing, but not beyond reach. We love you! All because of Jesus, Amen.

6.

The Open Door

Every fall Ken and I follow the University of Mississippi football team wherever they go. This is his passion, and since he is my greatest encourager, I am right beside him almost every game. I think he has missed only two games at home or away between 1992 and 2010.

He realizes that I do not fully share his football fervor, so he is very considerate of me on our little away-game trips. We eat well, travel well and sigh-see well. Many years ago, our schedule took us to historic New Orleans (before the devastation of Hurricane Katrina). We were there a couple of extra days, and during that time we shopped a little, walked a lot and taxed our digestive systems inordinately. I love architecture and Old World charm, so I drooled over the quaint streets, the multi-colored houses, the balconies, the wrought iron gates, the incredible doors with their individualized hardware and the hundreds of styles of shutters. All of this was blissful art to me. And, it would lead to my next game changer.

After a very full day, New Orleans-style, we retreated to our quaint little hotel room to retire for the evening, completely exhausted. That night I had a very vivid dream that I knew was a message from the Lord. In the dream I found myself standing before two massive French doors made of wood. The fronts of the doors were crafted with wood slats placed on the diagonal running the full length of the doors, with each diagonal strip perfectly lining up with its twin on the companion door. In my dream (or vision), as I gazed at the closed doors, I noticed that they were so tall that I could not see the tops. I then noticed that the door on my right had a handle, but the door on my left had none. I reasoned that I could open the door on the right because of its handle, but I could not open the door on the left. Suddenly, the door on the left – the one without the handle – opened, and a hand from inside reached out and took my hand and began to draw me inside. I then came to myself and began mentally trying to understand the message in the dream. As I lay in bed, I replayed the dream over and over in my head, feeling that a door would open to me that I could not open because of the no handle in the dream, yet, when it did open, I was to go inside. Whatever this assignment, it would be multi-faceted as evidenced by the many slats. And because of my not being able to see the tops, I would also never know the full extent of it.

I did not tell Ken or anyone else about the dream right away, but I did write it down, wondering if it would be days, weeks or possibly years before it became a reality.

Ken and I were continuing to go to the little Messianic Jewish Synagogue whenever possible. Many times I would go by myself because his job often demanded weekend hours – of course, strategically worked around football. I do not know how much time passed from that open-door dream until this particular Saturday morning, but it was not the years I had wondered if it might take. This particular Shabbat I went to the Synagogue alone and lost myself in the Jewish music, the Davidic dance, the Torah reading and watching the precious children following the Torah Scroll around the room as the Rabbi carried it for all the congregants to reach out and touch, expressing their love for God's Word. I so appreciated the way the Rabbi tied the Old Testament in with the New, and his tenderness toward Yeshua (the Hebrew name for Jesus, which means salvation). Shabbat services were my personal spiritual oasis.

After an inspiring morning of praise, worship and Bible study, we were dismissed. I proceeded to leave with my cup overflowing. The Rabbi was standing at the door shaking hands and greeting all attendees as we exited, and I gratefully reached out and shook his awaiting hand. (I am still in awe that Jews genuinely like us Gentiles. I do not know from where these feelings stem, but if you share them as well, I can tell you of a certainty that they are completely unfounded.) The Rabbi robustly grasped my hand and then said something that took me quite by surprise. He said, "Diane, I need to talk to you; can you give me a call sometime?" Did I hear him correctly? This Rabbi just asked for an appointment with me? Much to my dismay, I had to wait a couple of days because their offices are closed on Mondays to give them a two-day break. I had to wait three whole days before I could make that call.

Tuesday morning finally arrived, and it was all I could do to keep from calling at 8 a.m. sharp. I knew I needed to tone myself down a bit and try and not pounce on him before he made it into the office. So, leisurely, around 10:00, I phoned his office, and he took my call. We made that much-anticipated appointment date (for me, anyway), which was not soon enough.

I arrived a few minutes early on the scheduled date and was ushered into his office. After a little chit-chat, he began to tell me the purpose for the meeting. He explained that Israel would soon celebrate her fiftieth birthday since becoming a nation in 1948 and that the Lord had laid it on his heart that it was time for Christians to start blessing Jews. Then he said, "God told me to call you." What a Jewish game changer!

He continued by telling me that he could put me in touch with other like-minded Christians who also have a heart for Israel, and we could get together and decide on an appropriate gift to give our Memphis Jewish community from the local Christian community. Then he said, "Pray about this and let me know." I knew this was the door that I could not open, the one I had seen in my dream in New Orleans, and I also knew that I did not have to pray about it, but told him that I would. I wanted to tell him about the dream and why I was so confident about this assignment, but feared he might think I was crazy and take the whole thing back.

As I was sitting there on the couch in his office, I was inwardly floating on clouds with this wonderful new opportunity. Then, he began to strike a slight note of concern in me. He said, "Do not give them money, and do not just give them a proclamation; everyone gives them a proclamation. You need to do something that will genuinely express to the entire Jewish community a sincere appreciation for who they are and for the Nation of Israel." My initial thoughts were that this was going to be a piece of cake, never imagining the extent of this exciting new labor of love.

He gave me a list of a dozen or so people to contact, and I had my own list of close friends from church I definitely wanted involved. I took the list and skipped out of his office, oblivious to the possible twists and turns ahead for our soon-to-be-formed committee, and never once anticipating the stop signs, yield signs, no U-turns or dead ends that were to come. I was totally confident that the Lord had called, and what more was needed?

At this same time, I was months into the Tuesday night Hebrew classes and Naomi and I were becoming more and more comfortable with and dependent upon each other. Our relationship had developed into one that allowed for each of us to speak candidly to the other, and it was obvious to her that I was still quite green about Jewish matters, so this, thankfully, afforded me a great deal of leverage. She had to, and still does, forgive me for a lot. After my visit with the Rabbi, I immediately went to her house to tell her everything – the dream, the Rabbi's charge and the proposed new committee.

As I was driving there, I was intensely mulling over the gift we were supposed to give them, and could not wait to get Naomi's input. After all, she is an Israeli Jew – who better to help with the decision? I eagerly asked for her thoughts as to what we could give the Memphis Jewish community as a birthday gift from Christians, and she immediately replied, "Well, do not give them money because they will just build another bathroom on the Jewish Community Center." Then she said something that nearly took my breath away. She said, "Give them an ambulance." I said, "A what?" (Her husband is a doctor, so naturally her mind runs along such lines.) She said, "Give them an Israeli Red Cross ambulance." I said, "Can we do such a thing?" She said, "Of course you can." (Suddenly, all I could focus on were the dollar signs clicking off in my head, knowing that we did not have so much as a dime.)

"Well, how much does an ambulance cost," I asked. Her confident, matter-of-fact reply was, "I don't know, but you can raise it." It is just about this time that I began to second guess this thrilling new assignment. Oh, and do not forget about my hubby, Ken, who is a no-nonsense, staunch banker from the old school of finance. Can you imagine my going home and telling him that *we* are going to raise the money to buy an Israeli Red Cross ambulance? I think about this time I threw out every verse I ever learned about not worrying.

I phoned all of the people on the Rabbi's list, and those on my own personal list, and set our first meeting date – at the Messianic synagogue. I loved that. I had called our church to ask if the new committee, which had several members from that church, could hold its weekly meetings there to work on this project, and was told that they do not allow outside groups to use the facility. That was my first wake-up call. I then called the Jewish Community Center to ask if we could hold our meetings there, and they said the same thing, "No outside groups." We had to lean on the Rabbi from the little Messianic Synagogue, and he graciously consented to our meeting in their facility and even gave me my very own key. Unbelievable!

We held our first meeting and I was delighted at how well we all meshed together. We were from several different denominations, different ethnic groups and the age range was all across the board, but what a neat group of plain folk! The first thing I did was to ask the Rabbi if he would come to that start-up meeting and tell the whole group how all of this came to be. (I did tell them about my dream.) The Rabbi commissioned us, prayed over us and then took his leave, and the first meeting of Christian Friends of Israel – Memphis commenced.

Squirming in my seat, I told them about the conversation with Naomi and her suggestion of an ambulance. No one flinched! I wondered why they did not pick up their things and race for the door while they had their chance, but they completely embraced that first piece of the puzzle. George, who had been to Israel more than a dozen times, volunteered to research the ambulance company and find out the details and that all-important price tag. Others took on their assignments, such as how to involve area churches and Christian businesses, publicity, and so on, with the greatest committee of all being the absolutely imperative prayer team, comprised of Edith and Ruth. That first meeting went quite well.

Afterward, Naomi said I needed to go to the Memphis Jewish Federation and talk to the executive director there and tell him of our plans. She said she would make the arrangements and go with me, and I began to sense we were fast approaching the point of no return. The scheduled date arrived, and she and I both were escorted into his office where we sat at a small round table so I could lay out before him our Christian plans for celebrating Israel's fiftieth birthday.

(This executive director ((now a highly revered friend)) told me much later something of which I was completely unaware at the time of that initial meeting. He said he had moved to Memphis only two weeks prior to our meeting to take the lead position at the Memphis Jewish Federation, and he said that when this Christian came into his office with this proposition, he just knew it would be the demise of his promising new career.)

At one point in our conversation, it was as though God allowed me to see right through this man, and I intuitively knew he was wondering how I was going to turn all of this around and try to convert him. I instinctively knew this – it was truly uncanny. I vividly remember leaning across the table face-to-face with him and saying, "I know you think we are trying to convert you, but we aren't. The Bible says in Genesis 12:3 that God will bless those who bless Israel and He will curse those who curse her, and all I'm asking is for you to give us a chance to obey God's command." That was for me one of those defining God moments; it certainly was not pre-planned – the Lord gave me what I needed when I needed it, and He gave me the boldness with which to say it. That Scripture literally defused what I believe could easily have been the premature death of this new project. All suspicion began to fade. We relaxed back into our seats, and then Naomi told him our plans to give them an Israeli Red Cross ambulance. I told him this was God's assignment, and although we did not have the funds yet, we were confident He would take care of all the details. (All I had to do was to believe in my head what I KNEW in my heart was true and what my lips had declared.)

He very graciously, yet still somewhat a little reservedly, accepted our proposed gift offer, and we parted company with my giving him absolute assurance that we would not do anything without his prior approval, and that if at any time he was uncomfortable with anything, we would stop whatever it was immediately. We were at their service.

The meeting concluded and Naomi and I left feeling very confident that this initial first meeting with the Jewish community had gone quite well. She went on her merry way, and I was left with that ambulance albatross price tag ever weightier around my neck. "Oh," I wondered, "How is this ever going to play out?"

Trust in the Lord with all thine heart; and lean not unto thine own understanding. In all thy ways acknowledge him, and he shall direct thy paths. Proverbs 3:5-6.

Prayer: Father, thank you that we can trust your calling, even when the entire world screams to the contrary. And, thank you that we can "trust you, try you and prove you," and you even invite us to do it. The walk of faith is a lonely walk, but you have promised never to leave us or forsake us. And, in looking back over all these many years, it has been as you said it would be: You have never left and you have never forsaken. All praise and honor and glory be to the Only Wise God who can be trusted in every situation. I love you eternally because Jesus makes it possible. In His dear Name, Amen.

7.

God's Approach to Fundraising

Unrelenting alarm resonated throughout my whole being as I pondered our commitment to purchase the ambulance, and of my promising the Memphis Jewish Federation that we would make this presentation at their fiftieth birthday celebration for Israel – only six months away. As if my own personal faith battles were not enough, there was my husband's myriad of questions as to how *I* proposed to do this, and how *he* was going to come up with the $65,000 price tag. He pointed out (on numerous occasions) the obvious: Nobody knew our little group, we had no money collected, we did not have tax-exempt status and who was going to seriously contribute with a platform like that? He was not posing any obstacle that I had not already painfully considered myself. Half of me said, "This is the way faith works," and the other half said, "There is a fine line between faith and common sense."

Weeks passed with our committee continuing to meet and make plans to buy the ambulance, and doing everything we knew to do at the time. I read everyone's searching eyes each meeting as they looked at me for answers. Also, they could assuredly sense the consternation in Ken over this mammoth undertaking. Many times I would just want to be sick and run away.

But, at desperate times, God in His tenderness would send His little signature trademarks of encouragement, and these would prod me to plunge head long into the faith column. I remember one such occasion in particular. We were meeting weekly at the little Messianic Synagogue, which, you will recall had graciously entrusted me with a key. I arrived early for this particular meeting, as did a couple of the other ladies as well. I proceeded to retrieve the key from my purse so that we could go inside and set up, and suddenly realized that I had forgotten it. The meeting was scheduled to begin in about ten minutes, and I knew there was no time to go home and get back without holding everyone up considerably. I was sickened, and the ladies felt my agony and frustration.

One of the ladies headed out around the building, checking all the doors and windows in hopes that something had been left unlocked. All was shut tight. I knew Ken was going to be further exasperated with me and my role in this. How could the chairperson forget something as vital as the key? Others began arriving, Ken being one of them, and he said to me, along with that look, "I can't believe you didn't check to see if you had the key before you left." I did wonder why on earth God put me, of all people, in this role. Just about that time, Edith, one of the ladies who co-chairs our prayer group and who is a true prayer warrior, took out her house key and walked up to a side entrance door that leads directly into the worship area of the Synagogue and said, "In the Name of Jesus," and pushed her key into the lock, turned it and opened the door, while the rest of us stood there in total shock. What so astounded me was that I knew this door was never used. Only God could have engineered that. After gathering our composure, and our materials, we all went inside with the absolute assurance that we were about God's business and were right where we were supposed to be.

Our little committee's plan of attack encompassed the predictably standard approach of contacting churches, using radio and TV and drawing from mission groups that had a heart for Israel. We knew realistically, though, that none of these would produce the $65,000-plus price tag needed for the ambulance, not to mention the additional funds necessary for publicity, office supplies, mailings, etc. Prayers for the how-to's of this venture never ceased, and calls to our two-person prayer team seemed to be phoned in daily.

One day I was visiting at Naomi's house (who had counseled us to buy the ambulance as our gift) and fervently wishing that she would somehow come up with a plan for us to raise these funds. After all, the ambulance was her idea! To me she seemed a little flippant with her response. It was always the same, "It's not that much money; you'll figure it out." As far as I was concerned, it might as well have been a million dollars, and we were getting down to crunch time. How do nobodies come up with tens of thousands of dollars? The odds were definitely not in our favor.

As I left Naomi's house that day, I was begging and pleading with every fiber of my being for the Lord to drop the money from the sky, let it grow on trees, or whatever means He could devise, so that we could order the ambulance, and not to mention so we could save face with both the Christian and Jewish communities. I prayed in absolute desperation. Suddenly, I spotted some books in the middle of the street. I quickly scoped the landscape and realized that I was approaching one of the largest Synagogues in Memphis, and surmised that these were possibly Jewish books. My mind played out the obvious-to-me scenario: they belonged to a Jewish person who had dropped them on their way to or from Synagogue, their names would assuredly be inside and I would get to befriend a new Jewish person. (I can be so dramatic.)

To my initial dismay, there were no names written inside for me to contact, but, rather, the treasures I retrieved from the street were three identical booklets. On closer scrutiny, I realized these were Jewish memorial booklets, with the Hebrew date of 5748 (1988) on the front, and entitled, *Book of Remembrance*. As I scanned the pages, it became quickly apparent that money had been raised with these little booklets. The first few pages were full-page memorials with fancy gold borders. The next few were also full-page memorials with blue borders. Next came half-pages with blue borders, then quarter-pages with blue borders, and last were single-line listings.

Every excitable emotion suddenly came to life inside me because I realized that what I was holding in my hand was God's design for our raising the money for the ambulance. This was definitely a Jewish game changer! We would use the same format, but rather than containing memorials, ours would carry tributes to Jewish friends, neighbors, doctors, lawyers, accountants, and so on, from Christians! While theirs were booklets of sad, possibly painful memories, ours would be booklets of hope, respect, tribute and unconditional love. Our full pages with gold borders would sell for a $1,000 each; our full blue pages – $500; half pages – $250; quarter pages – $125; and single-line listings would be for any amount.

We sincerely wanted each participant to be a part of this project and to receive something in return for their contribution, and this they did. Each donor was given the privilege of writing his or her own personal blessing or note of appreciation to their Jewish honoree, with each tribute showing the recipient's name, as well as the donor's. Praise God for hearing our cries and for giving us such a unique (Jewish at that – so like God) way to raise the necessary funds while simultaneously blessing our local Jewish people. That is fundraising at its best!

The committee was ecstatic with the new plan, knowing without a doubt that it was God's Master Mind. God, of a certainty, was behind all of this; He had a definite plan of attack – a plan that had a curiously comfortable Jewish feel to it and which He chose to interject into our willing, Christian strategizing. Our theme was "acting locally" (Memphis), "impacting globally" (Israel).

There were about six months between the time we held our first meeting and our target date for Israel's fiftieth celebration of their independence (1948-1998), and, Praise God, we reached our goal. Our little copycat booklets contained forty full gold pages, in addition to the numerous other pages. We raised all of the $65,000 needed for the ambulance, plus the additional funds necessary to run the campaign, and, amazingly, had money left over. What a victory for all involved, and what a worthy tribute to our Jewish community!

(There was a tragedy along the way that God turned into a blessing. Mary Jane, one of the committee members, and one of my dearest friends, lost her mother during this time, and she joyfully used much of her inheritance to purchase gold pages of tribute for many of her Jewish doctor friends and acquaintances. Such selfless acts do not go unnoticed by the Lord.)

We worked with the American Red Magen David for Israel ambulance service, which had the vehicle built to Israeli specifications. It was fully equipped, and we were told that it was state-of-the-art, and should the need arise, surgeries could be performed inside. This company was tremendously accommodating to us Christians, and their representatives were always sensitive to our monetary restraints.

We were allowed to put an inscription on the front door of the ambulance, and chose: "Presented to the People of Israel In Honor of THE MEMPHIS JEWISH CITIZENS By THE MEMPHIS AND

MID-SOUTH CHRISTIAN COMMUNITY, Memphis, Tennessee, U.S.A., 3 IYAR 5758" (the Hebrew date).

The ambulance was delivered to Memphis for presentation at the Synagogue where their birthday celebration was held. It remained in town for about two weeks, during which time we stationed it at each Synagogue for a couple days to show off, and also delivered extra tribute booklets to each of those synagogues so that their members would see the names of the Christians funding the ambulance and could read the personalized tribute messages.

I recall with such warmth the day the ambulance arrived. Its first stop was the Memphis Jewish Community Center, and most of the committee members were there anxiously awaiting their first look. The ladies who made up our prayer team brought anointing oil and anointed it inside and out. At one point we all piled inside and had a prayer and praise celebration because of the faithfulness of Almighty God.

After those two weeks, their little ambulance that we had come to love so dearly was shipped to Ein Gedi, Israel, to serve the Jewish people there. (George, from our committee, has since been back to Israel and scouted around and actually found our beloved gift in action.)

Can there be any doubt that God loves His Church blessing His Chosen People? He certainly made believers out of the fourteen of us. But, what is so heart-wrenching in all of this is that by and large His Church is completely hands-off where Israel and the Jews are concerned. Oh, how this must grieve the heart of Almighty God! As I ponder this, I am reminded that the true Church is comprised of individuals, and if our religious institutions refuse to embrace the Jewish roots of our faith, then may the Lord draw out those who will boldly say, *"Though none go with me, still I will follow."*

> *Also I heard the voice of the Lord, saying, Whom shall I send, and who will go for us? Then said I, Here am I; send me.* Isaiah 6:8

Prayer: Oh, Lord, how our hearts break at the ignorance of the Church concerning your place for Israel! You have laid your heart bare in your Word about your relationship with her; yet, in ignorance many in your Church have now transferred her position to the Church! What a travesty! Oh, how this must grieve you through and through – your two loves: the Chosen and the Church in a tug-of-war for position! Lord, may it not be so! Rather, let us realize that your heart is God-sized, and there is lovingly room for both. Please forgive our prideful elevation of self, and let us be imitators of Christ and of His servant attitude. Father, chip away at our stony hearts and restore those hearts that are pliable and teachable and void of devilish pride. Oh, Lord God Almighty, have mercy and have pardon. Reclaim what the enemy has viciously tried to steal. For all eternity we will praise you for your great mercy and for your boundless grace! In the incomparable Name of Jesus, Amen.

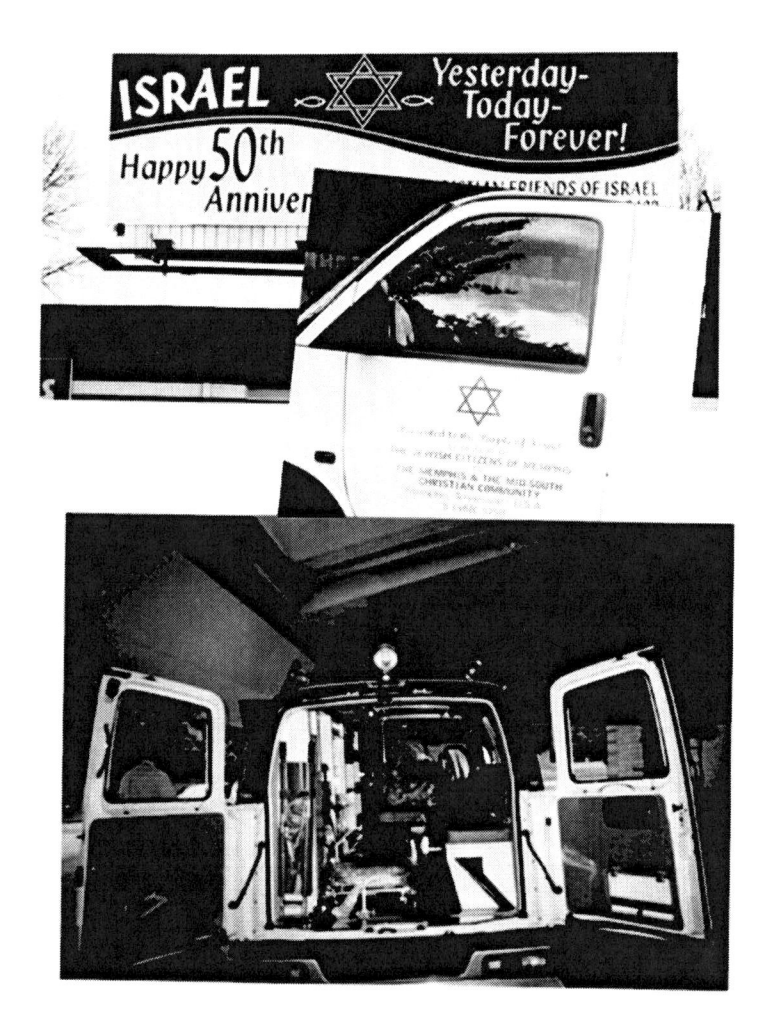

Picture of Ambulance Door

Fundraising Booklet

8.

Elvis's Love for the Jews ... and More

I continued to be amazed at the ease with which I traversed between the two realms of Christianity and Judaism. Although for a Christian to venture into the Jewish world is generally considered off-limits, even taboo, it felt so comfortable and so natural. It was as if I were finally fulfilling a deep, inner longing that had lain dormant.

The Jewish ladies in our Hebrew class were fast becoming my dear friends. They never tried to coax me out of my faith or diminish my zeal for the Lord. Genuine love existed between us; I can truthfully say it was unconditional love. I was not on some kind of covert mission to convert them; I was simply about my Father's business – on my own pursuit of unity between His Chosen and this grateful Christian.

However, there was one time, about which I must tell you, where there was talk of conversion.

Naomi, my dear friend and Hebrew teacher, and I were in the car on one of our many outings together. We were having an interesting conversation, which usually meant that she was talking and I was hanging on to every word. Amazingly, the conversation turned to Elvis Presley. She was saying how she loved his music. Her personal favorite was *Amazing Grace*. I chuckled on the inside thinking, "How interesting." Then, she said, "Did you know that Elvis Presley loved the Jews?" I had lived in Memphis for probably thirty years and had never before heard that. She had only moved to the city a short while back – long after Elvis had died. I asked inquisitively, "How do you know that?" She told the story, which I am sure continues to circulate in Memphis Jewish circles. She said that one day Elvis rode his motorcycle to the Memphis Jewish Community Center and gave them a check for $5,000 (an impressive sum at the time) just because. That gesture (which I am sure he could easily afford), spoke volumes to them. It was an unsolicited, voluntary act of kindness, expecting nothing in return. It was his genuine expression of unconditional love, and probably all 10,000 Jews in the Memphis area know the story.

It brought back to my mind the time I visited Graceland (his home and now a museum), and being shocked to see in Elvis's trophy room a massive (bordering on gaudy) gold necklace with the Hebrew letters *chet* and *yod* hanging from the heavy chain. These two letters combine to make the word *chai*, which is *life* in Hebrew, a very important Jewish word. Elvis Presley had a Jewish necklace!

I was musing over all of this when suddenly Naomi blurted out, "Diane, I would love to convert you, but I can't." The part that most intrigued me was, ". . . but I can't." Very curious, I said, "Why can't you?" Her answer continues to astound me; it impacts me as much today writing it as it did the day she spoke it. Her simple, yet profound, reply was, "Because conversion is in the heart, and only God can touch the heart." What unparalleled wisdom! Although she may not consider herself religious, her knowledge and understanding of conversion far outpaces that of most active, committed evangelicals. Of course she cannot convert me, any more than I can convert her. I loved and embraced this latest Jewish game changer.

(When reading through the preliminary manuscript of this book, Naomi wanted to make sure that I understood and added to this writing that in Judaism a person is not allowed to convert merely for external reasons, but it must come from a true inner belief and a genuine sincerity that he or she wants to become a Jew. She also told me that in Orthodox Judaism this procedure takes a year of study and deeds, culminating in an open council before God and before all Holy people of the Jewish community.)

Another story in that same vein is sadly the flip side. One Sunday morning just before the church service, I was donning my choir robe and doing the other perfunctory things we women do before entering the worship service. I was in the back hall, not yet in position, when another choir member came dashing up to me in somewhat of a frenzy and said, "Diane, I have a new boss, and she's Jewish; how do I convert her?" It caught me so off guard that I had to tell her I would get back to her. After she left and I collected my thoughts, I pondered, How did we come to this mindset? Where was the same reverential fear of, "Conversion is in the heart and only God can touch the heart?" Who put us under this bondage? I was deeply grieved in my spirit, realizing that she is a fair representation of the Church as a whole.

She and I are both altos and were sitting next to each other that particular Sunday morning. I told her that she must first learn about Judaism, and there are no instant crash courses. I gave her two simple tasks. I explained that Hanukkah was soon approaching, and suggested she buy a greeting card and send it to her new Jewish supervisor wishing her a happy holiday. Then, I explained to her the Jewish reverence for the Sabbath, and taught her the simple little Sabbath greeting that she could say to her "new boss" each Friday upon leaving work: "Shabbat Shalom" (Sabbath peace). I also told her to love this Jewish person unconditionally, something few grasp. I said that if God should give her an open door (and there is no mistaking God's open doors) to talk about Yeshua (the Hebrew name for Jesus, which means salvation), then she was absolutely free to enter, but cautioned her against going through a door God had not opened. Doors we force open actually give entrance to the enemy, something no Christian wants or can afford. On a couple of occasions afterward, I asked how the new relationship was progressing, and could tell the zeal had waned. I was saddened at the lost opportunity for both of them.

Let me share with you my own experience of a time I believe was an open door when conversion did come up with another Jewish friend. This lady's name is Sylvia, and she was in her late eighties at the time. I do not recall how we met, but she was a very interesting and colorful individual. I visited in her home a couple of times, and occasionally she and I would go out to lunch together. She told me many fascinating stories, including one about the time she attended a little Baptist church for a while and even sang in the choir. She said she loved that church and loved singing those hymns. That so amazed me – a non-believing Jew singing hymns about Jesus in an evangelical church. She was without a doubt the exception to the rule.

As she was so open spiritually, I invited her to attend the little Messianic Jewish Synagogue with me where I occasionally worshipped on Saturday mornings. She was delighted for the opportunity to get out (she no longer drove), and gladly took me up on the offer. I wondered what was going through her mind as these Jewish people joyfully paraded around the sanctuary following the Rabbi who was holding the Torah Scroll, or when they sang Hebrew songs about Yeshua. Did these possibly conjure up early childhood memories of going to Synagogue with her parents? Or, did she perhaps process the similarities of that little Baptist Church and the same teachings in this Messianic Synagogue? As peculiar as it may seem, I actually think that bringing Jesus into the Jewish setting made her incredibly uncomfortable. It was okay to talk about Him in that little Baptist Church, but it was soon apparent that to bring this same Jesus into a Jewish religious service was more than she could bear.

One day as she and I were discussing the Jewishness of Christianity, she blurted out, "I loved my parents more than anything, and they did not believe in Jesus, so if they are in hell, I would rather go to hell and be with them than to live in heaven without them." I knew from such an outburst that somewhere in her past someone had told her that if her parents did not believe in Jesus, they would go to hell. Her relegation of God to second place shook me to the very core of my being. I replied something like, "Sylvia, you know you would rather be with God in Heaven," to which she emphatically reiterated that she would rather spend eternity in hell with her parents. It quickly became apparent that this conversation was extremely upsetting to her. However, I felt that her statement about preference for her parents over God qualified as an open door.

I genuinely had not tried to convert any of these precious people, leaving that entirely up to the Lord, but, oh, how it grieved me her saying that she would rather spend eternity in hell with her parents than in Heaven with God. She was actually breaking one of the Ten Commandments: "Thou shalt have no other gods before me." I knew she was speaking out of ignorance and could never mean such a thing. It brought to light her true relationship with the Lord. Sylvia was so visibly shaken by the conversation, though, that I also knew I had to leave it alone; no good could come from pursuing it. However, I did determine to write her a letter from a biblical perspective using only Old Testament Scripture about her choosing parents over God.

The following day, December 15, 1999, I wrote Sylvia and told her how much I loved her, how I loved being with her and loved her zeal for life, but that I could not get out of my mind the previous day's conversation. I spoke about the *shema*, which Jews chant every Sabbath: "Hear O Israel, the Lord is our God, the Lord is one." (For most Jews this verse is the great divide, because if the Lord God is one, then how can we say that Jesus is the Son of God and is equally God?)

I explained that I had discovered in my Hebrew class that Elohim (God's Name in Scripture) is a plural word, and then quoted Isaiah 9:6, where it says that to us a child is born ... and the child's name is Mighty God and Everlasting Father. I also quoted Proverbs 30:4, where it is obviously speaking of God, and concludes with, "What is his name, and the name of his son? Tell me if you know?"

I wrote out all of Isaiah 53:1-11, and underscored the portions where it says He was pierced for our transgressions and by His stripes we are healed; how the Lord laid on Him the iniquity of us all; and that for the transgression of *my* people he was stricken.

I mentioned again how grievous it was that she would choose her parents over God, and ended with what God requires in order for us to be redeemed. It was a lengthy letter, but I felt that to the best of my ability I had covered everything known to me. I prayed fervently over that letter and then mailed it, entrusting it to the Lord.

Three days after receiving the letter, Sylvia phoned me to say that she had not slept day or night since the letter arrived. (I do not think it was as much my letter as it was the impact of her own testimony.) She said she had read and re-read it over and over. She said she had a nephew who was a cantor (music director) at one of the local synagogues, and she took it to him. He read the letter and told her that she was never to speak of religion to a Christian again.

Sadly, Sylvia died shortly after that. Oh, how I prayed that before her death she understood and embraced God's plan of salvation, and that one day I will see her worshipping before The Almighty's throne in total adoration of His worthiness.

I guess one of the things that I find most perplexing with God's Chosen People is their lack of desire to read God's Word. One night our Hebrew class was out celebrating our teacher's birthday. One of the members in the class had a van large enough to accommodate everyone, so we were all together headed for the restaurant when one of the ladies took command of the conversation and went from person to person asking, "Do you read your Bible every day?" I was embarrassed because I knew where she was going with this. Each of the ladies replied, "No," and then last of all she came to me and then answered for me. She said, "Diane does." The point I am making is that we think all Jews know the Scriptures better than we do, but actually, the reverse is probably more nearly correct.

It is for certain that Jesus is all throughout the Scriptures, Old and New, but if you are not in the Word, how will you ever find Him? You cannot – unless you see Him being lived out in another's life? A Christian may be the only "Bible" others read.

There's one more heartbreaking story I want to share. Ken and I received an invitation to attend a Sukkot (Feast of Tabernacles/Booths/Ingathering) celebration at the home of a local Rabbi. This particular Rabbi does not have a synagogue but has a religious ministry, and thus the title of Rabbi. We had never before met him, but he had heard of some of our Jewish-Christian involvement, and he was interested in a possible working relationship, hence the invitation. We were elated to be included, but understandably a little reserved because we did not know him.

(Sukkot is the last of the seven Jewish, biblical feasts and is a joyous holiday. It centers around and celebrates all the harvest being gathered in and the time for enjoying the fruits of one's labor. For seven days families take their meals, and oftentimes sleep outside underneath the stars, in their outdoor sukkah, or shelter, ((singular for sukkot)), reminiscing about God's faithfulness in the wilderness wanderings, His faithfulness in bringing them to the Promised Land, and His continued faithfulness in their daily lives.)

Ken was seated directly to the Rabbi's left, and I was to the left of Ken. We had front-row seats and thoroughly enjoyed the teaching and having a better understanding of this Feast and of its relevance for today. It was a delightful evening, and we found this family very charming. They have six sons, one of whom was in Israel serving in the Israeli Defense Force.

At the conclusion of the fabulous meal and the interesting teaching and conversation, people began to take their leave, but the Rabbi held Ken and me in further conversation. I loved the one-on-

one. By that time, several of his sons had gathered around the head of the table, and I was captivated by each of their outgoing personalities. From my vantage point, it was a picture-perfect family. They were all extremely intelligent, and for young men of their ages, they were posing some highly intellectual, philosophical questions. One of them commented about something spiritual, and I replied with something like, "Well, the Bible says . . ." He immediately took control of the conversation and said with authority and a somewhat superior demeanor, "We are not allowed to read the Bible in our home," going on to explain that the commentaries by the Jewish sages are the more reliable and much preferred sources. I know the shock of his saying that the Bible was not allowed to be read in their home must have registered from the top of my head to the soles of my feet, because our extended session with the Rabbi ended quite abruptly, and we were rather hastily dismissed, even though neither Ken nor I had said a single word. I am sure by our expressions that we probably did not need to.

If that brought alarm to me, what must such things do to the heart of Almighty God? But, does He throw up His hands and quit? Did He throw up His hands and quit with you? He certainly did not with me. He loves His Chosen People to the death. He has an eternal covenant with them. He is not quitting, and neither can we. Was this also a Jewish game changer for me? Probably sadly so, but I would have to say that the game it changed was to underscore for me the need to pray more fervently. Oh, dear friend, do not use such experiences as the opportunity to judge or condemn. Let us not forget that it was this Rabbi's ancestry that faithfully preserved and recorded the Scriptures for you and me today. Before judging such a scenario, let us look deeply into our own lives and our obvious love, or quite possibly lack thereof, of the Scriptures. Is there really room to boast?

There is a heavenly Sukkot awaiting us where one day all will be gathered in and where there will be the greatest of all celebrations. Let us faithfully stay the course – loving unconditionally – because we definitely do not want to miss out in our playing a part in that final, joyous Ingathering!

I bring near my righteousness; it shall not be far off, and my salvation shall not tarry: and I will place salvation in Zion for Israel my glory. Isaiah 46:13

Prayer: Father, my heart wants to break in two becuse of man's ignorance – especially mine. Oh, how we must grieve you when we choose our own way. I know I have grieved you over and over, even though you have invested your All in me. Please forgive me for the many, many times that I have displayed a detestable, superior attitude. God, without you, I am nothing! That is the truth, the whole truth, and nothing but the truth! All of my righteousness is as filthy rags – but, praise your Holy Name, you did not leave me in that hopeless state. Thank you that, on Calvary, you exchanged your righteousness for my filthy rags. You made a way, where, apart from you, there was absolutely no way. To you be all superiority, praise and awe. Humbly, in the Name of Jesus I pray, Amen.

9.

A Visit with the Rabbi

There were many Jewish stories during the ten years of my writing *Ruth 3,000 Years of Sleeping Prophecy Awakened*, but one in particular will always stand out. It comes to mind often, and I wonder if some day that scene might again be revisited.

In the initial stages of writing Ruth, I had many questions with virtually no answers. I was intrigued with the multiples of things the Lord seemed to be depositing into my world, all stamped with "Jewish", so I always gravitated in that direction when working on the Book of Ruth. One day as I was poring over my writings and frustrated with the volume of loose ends, I had the brainstorm to call one of the local synagogues and ask if their Rabbi might give me an appointment so I could ask him about all the many unknowns.

A part of me said: You've got to be crazy; you can't even get in to see most pastors – and you think a Rabbi will see you? But the other side said, I've been rejected many times and another won't hurt. How will I ever know if I don't try? There are several synagogues in the Memphis area from the very Orthodox to the more liberal Reform congregations. I wanted the most observant Rabbi fielding my questions, so I chose the Orthodox synagogue.

Needless to say, even though I was committed to making the call, I was petrified. Who was I to presume to do such a thing? I had never been to that synagogue and did not even know where it was. It was blind faith. I called and spoke with the receptionist. I told her the purpose for my call: I was doing a Bible study on Ruth and wanted to ask the Rabbi some questions about my study. Needless to say she was a little reluctant and told me she would speak with him and call me back. She phoned the next day to say that he would see me and gave me the appointment time. I was amazed at such an opportunity extended to a Gentile female homemaker from an Orthodox rabbi.

The meeting date arrived and I was punctual with my list of questions in hand. Since I love baking, I also thought it would be a goodwill gesture to make him a fresh loaf of bread as my way of saying "thank you."

I entered the synagogue and located the receptionist. She then directed me to his administrative assistant where I waited until I was summoned. A few minutes later I was ushered into the Rabbi's office.

I was greeted by a very warm and inviting middle-aged man whose office was filled with books and whose desk was a bit disheveled. He motioned for me to take a seat directly across from him, and there we sat face-to-face.

My insides were churning. Oh, how I had prayed before coming to this time and place. I was most assuredly out of my element, but what I keenly understood was that I was granted an extraordinary favor that was truly undeserved.

The Rabbi tried to put me at ease with light conversation about the weather and Memphis, etc. Then, he asked the purpose for my visit. I relayed to him that I was doing a study on Ruth (never mentioning I was actually writing a book) and had numerous unanswered questions and felt that a Jewish Rabbi would hold answers not available anywhere else. I pulled out my page of questions ready to go over them one-by-one, and trusting my once good shorthand to record the answers so as not to take up too much of his time. He walked around the desk and peered over my shoulder at the list and then walked back behind his desk to a bookcase on his back wall. He pulled out a small book on Ruth and handed it to me. (The Book of Ruth/Megillas Ruth, ArtScroll Tanach Series, a traditional commentary on the Books of the Bible, Rabbis Nosson Scherman/Meir Zlotowitz, General Editors, Mesorah Publications, ltd., 1989.) He asked if I knew how to use a Hebrew book, to which I replied, "No." He opened the book, from back to front. As he flipped the pages, he came to the term "The Name" and asked if I knew what it meant. "I did not," I answered. He said that in Jewish writings the names of God are never written but instead they use "The Name" so as not to write the Holy Names of God. He then said, "Return the book when you're finished."

Needless to say, I was grateful for the mini-Hebrew lesson but somewhat disappointed that I was not going to be able to ask him my questions. However, I think what most astonished me was that a prestigious Rabbi would loan an unknown Gentile woman a volume from his personal library merely with, "Return it when you're finished."

He took his seat again, reclining back, resuming the casual conversation. I handed him the loaf of homemade bread. He graciously accepted it but told me he could not keep it for himself because he observes kosher and it was not prepared in a kosher kitchen. I was a little embarrassed, but he quickly put me at ease understanding my lack of knowledge of such things. He said that he had a very good Gentile friend who was always more than happy to take such gifts off his hand.

He then changed the subject to what is this chapter's Jewish game changer. I do not recall the specific topic of conversation at the time, but seemingly out of nowhere, the Rabbi declared, "I know my son is not the Messiah". You have no idea the shock that rose up inside me. Those words sent all my emotions reeling. I was so stunned that I genuinely hoped my face did not register my internal alarm. He went on to say that his family is from the Tribe of Benjamin, and that Messiah will come from the Tribe of Judah, so he knew his son is not the Messiah.

It had never occurred to me that if you do not believe Messiah has come then you are looking for Him in every Jewish son born from the Tribe of Judah. And, interestingly, this same topic comes up in the Book of Ruth. In Ruth 3:11, it states: "… for all the city of my people doth know that thou art a virtuous woman." In a marriage involving a man from the Tribe of Judah (as was Boaz), the intended wife mattered a great deal because each union held the potential of producing the Messiah (which the Boaz/Ruth union ultimately did).

What is past history for us is great anticipation for the Jews, and God allowed me a personal peek into their eager expectation. It has been told to me on several occasions that Teddy Kollek, the late mayor of Jerusalem, once said: "When the Messiah comes we will ask, 'Sir, is this your first time here or your second?'"

I would like to close with one charge to you: "Don't miss opportunities!" Don't let your assessment of your "inferiority" dictate what you can and cannot do. Let God alone be the judge of that. You pray, trust Him and go through any door He opens to you.

> *I am sought of them that asked not for me; I am found of them that sought me not: I said, Behold me, behold me, unto a nation that was not called by my name.* Isaiah 65:1

Prayer: Oh, Father, how we must quench your Spirit because we have already pre-determined that we are not good enough to do this or that. God, please let us leave such decisions to you alone, and let us grab hold of the absolute fact that we are sons and daughters of the Most High God. We are not paupers of the Kingdom; we are ruling and reigning princes and princesses; we are (astonishingly) joint heirs with Christ! Let us refuse ever again to see ourselves as the world dictates but only to view ourselves through "thus saith the Lord" from the eternal Scriptures. Thank you, Lord, for this coveted position. To you alone be praise and adoration, world without end. In the incomparable Name that is above every name, Jesus, Amen.

10.

A New Twist on Kosher

I was thoroughly enjoying the privilege of living in my two worlds – my Christian world, and my new-found, somewhat complex Jewish world. There was so much to learn in that latter domain, and I wanted to grab hold of as much as possible.

Naomi and I talked nearly every day and saw each other as often as we could. Ken's and my two older sons were grown and gone, and the third was in high school. Hers were in middle school and high school. I had always heard that Jewish mothers pushed their children, and I was seeing it firsthand. I would worry how mine would function the next day if they were up past 10:00, but that was not the case in their home. They were urged to stay up as long as it took in order to be fully prepared for the next day's tests. There was no down time when it came to studies. The quest for education was as intense as anything I had ever witnessed.

I remember one day in particular that one of the girls had a very difficult test ahead of her, and Naomi was stressed. As this daughter left for class, Naomi insistently called after her, "Don't forget to kiss the mezuzah!" (This is the little box containing Scripture that God commanded the Jewish people to attach to the doorposts of their homes – thus putting His Word and Name on their homes, Deuteronomy 6:4-9.) Every means was exhausted for the sake of grades. But, let me follow all of this by saying that both of their daughters are now highly prestigious doctors; her driving forces yielded the desired outcome.

I did love being in their home – lots of tension, lots of drama. There was such a stark contrast between their home with daughters and ours with sons. I was rarely there when her husband was home, though; I had my own responsibilities in my own home, and I did not want to wear out my welcome. It was usually in the middle of the day that Naomi and I had our times together, and I cherished every moment.

The new twist to kosher and my next game changer came one day when Naomi and I were having lunch out together. This opportunity did not present itself very often because her girls would be in and out during the day in between classes at their private school. However, on this particular day, we had a delightful lunch planned at one of Ken's and my favorite restaurants. It is somewhat upscale, so we frequent it only on special occasions. The day was spectacular – perfect weather with lots of sunshine. I do not recall whether it was a special occasion, but it very well may have been one of our spring birthdays. As we entered the restaurant, I noticed a side door leading to the outside standing open. The hostess asked whether we wanted to sit inside or out. I was not aware they had outside seating, but with a day like this, there was no question as to which it would be.

We went through the open side door, descended a small flight of steps and followed our hostess across old brick pavers covered by overhanging trees and surrounded by several varieties of mature, flowering shrubs. We were seated at a round, wrought-iron table, and our waitress soon appeared to ask for our drink orders. (As much as I loved this new chapter in my life and being immersed in the Jewish world, I always treaded cautiously, keenly aware that I must never be a stumbling block in the path of God's Chosen People. I did not push through this new world without serious consideration for every word uttered and every deed done. I truly had a new appreciation for praying without ceasing. I prayed about everything, all the time, never wanting to be a hindrance to God dealing with His precious people. "God forbid that I should be a stumbling block!")

We studied our menus with all of its delectable, mouth-watering temptations. I felt as though I were queen for a day. The waitress arrived to take our orders, and Naomi chose the chef's special shrimp dish. When that came out of her mouth, there was intense grieving in my Spirit that she would order what God calls unclean and what the Jews were specifically commanded not to eat. I was crushed to the core. I cannot tell you why I felt this overpowering burden – except that I believe God was allowing me to experience His hurt.

What had begun as a picture-perfect day was now a huge knot in the pit of my stomach. And, please do not think that I have never disobeyed God – often deliberately; the times are without number, but there was much more operating that day than I could understand. I had seen Naomi eat shrimp on other occasions, and those times never bothered me, but this one was entirely different. This was far beyond me.

I do not know why I then said what I did, but it came out – in my spirit. I told God in that instant that whether or not she chose to eat kosher, I would do it for her. That was a huge turning point in my life, and I sincerely meant every word of it. I did not know that much about kosher, but from that moment on, this Christian was eating kosher. And, I know your religious wheels are probably turning like crazy right now about how you cannot do that for another, and where in the Bible does it give such a command, and all the other things that I can assure you in that split second went through my mind as well. I know it does not compute, but I also know what was in my spirit; I know the anguish I was feeling, and I know I embraced what was presented to me – what I was convicted to do. The decision was made, and there was no turning back.

I did not tell Naomi what happened that day; it was between God and me. It may have been because of her that I was now on this uncharted kosher course, but I can assure you, it was far beyond her by now; it was my commitment to God Almighty.

It has been a very interesting journey, to say the least, yet there have been so many affirmations along the way that I have never second guessed my resolve.

You can imagine my explaining all of this to Ken, right? He probably thought it would go away after a while, but he has seen God's hand in it almost as clearly as I have, and he does not give me grief over it any longer.

I do want to clarify the way I eat kosher. In Jewish circles there are many avenues for observing this command, some very simple, some extremely complex. My definition of kosher is what God spelled out in His Word in Genesis 9:4; Leviticus 11; and Deuteronomy 14:1-21. I do not eat the foods He calls unclean, and to put it simply and in the words of another dear Jewish friend: "no pork, no shellfish and no catfish." Of course, there are other specifics, but most of these typically do not come into play in our modern American diets (such as no camel, eagle, vulture, stork, owl, snake, alligator . . .).

I cannot tell you the times that we have gone out to eat with me wondering how in the world God was going to work around my eating kosher. Plus, I despise my eating choices being a topic for discussion. Trying to explain this gets a little tricky, as you can imagine. I know my eating kosher makes no sense, so I simply choose not to go there. I just want to go out to eat, order what I want to order, and let everyone else do the same, and let that be the end of the matter.

I remember one time when Ken and I were going to one of Memphis's famed barbecue restaurants, The Rendezvous. We were with another couple who did not know about my little eating oddity, and I was wondering how God was going to pull this one off this time. The menu there is somewhat limited, and the only things I knew they served were pork barbecue and ribs. I prayed and said, "God, I do not know how you are going to do this one, but I am leaving it in your hands."

We arrived and were escorted to our seats and given our menus, and to my delight, I discovered lamb riblets and barbecued beef on the menu. Not only would I be eating, and eating well, but I had choices. I love lamb and would never have imagined it being served at this world-renowned pork barbecue restaurant. Oh, how I delighted in God's little surprise that night!

Years after my diet change, Ken and I made a trip to south Florida to visit Naomi and her husband, who had relocated there in order for him to begin his own medical practice. That first night, they wanted to take us out to one of their favorite restaurants, a Middle Eastern establishment, complete with belly dancers. During the conversation, Naomi's husband turned to me and said, "Diane, why don't you eat pork?" I do not recall ever talking to Naomi about what happened to me that day in Memphis, and his question sent my head into a spin. It was not something I was comfortable discussing, and certainly not with Jewish people. However, before I could answer, Naomi turned to him and said, "She eats kosher for me because I won't." She caught me completely off-guard. I do not recall ever having said that to her. How did she know that? I cannot remember what I came back with after her response, but what I do remember is that she knew without my ever having said a word. (There is probably a tremendous spiritual lesson here.) Incredibly, though, my twist to kosher did not end there; years later, it would take yet another giant leap.

As mentioned previously, my dear, precious husband is an avid Ole Miss (the University of Mississippi) football fan. I do not even want to know which position she holds in his heart.

Game day at Oxford is a spectacle! It is probably the most outlandish extravagance on any college campus anywhere in America. Tailgating is redefined at Ole Miss. There is the mad dash at sundown the evening before to set up the personalized tents in "your" spot, the hours of food preparation, bouquets of live flowers, decorations, and on and on. There is no sense of satisfaction. Each game must be bigger and better than the one before.

You arrive early (around 7 a.m, no matter the game time), finish the setup and then mill around visiting and being visited. There is such excitement and hype! It is truly incredible! Tickets are a premium. If you happen to have good seats, you hold on to them, pay those yearly dues, and enjoy the fruits of your labor. It is as though you have two families: your own at-home family and your adopted football family. You genuinely get to know the folks tailgating around you and those sitting in the stadium seats next to you, and you look forward to seeing them year after year.

Early in our days of getting caught up in this obsession, we became acquainted with the man who had the seat next to Ken. His name is Jacob, and when I heard his last name, I knew he had to be Jewish. How impossible is it to be in this small, Southern college town, probably with only a couple of Jewish families, and we just happen to be sitting next to one of them? I asked Jacob if he was Jewish, and he seemed a little hesitant to respond, but told me that, yes, he was. I told him that God had given me an enormous love and respect for the Jewish people, and it was an honor to meet him. He was not impressed, probably a little bored, but as time went on, he warmed up to me, but he loved Ken! They were like "rah-rah" buddies, hollering and carrying on, and even at times keeping each other (fifty and sixty-year-old men) out of fights. (I will never understand this football thing.)

Jacob tailgated with a large group from Oxford, and we loved going by their setup before games to speak to him and see what they had cooking on their gigantic, over-sized grill. What a spectacle we all made of ourselves!

I remember that one particular game day was also the Jewish holiday, Rosh Hashanah, (Jewish New Year), and I had memorized the Hebrew blessing that they say to each other on this holiday. I said it to Jacob: "*La shanah tovah tik-a-te-vous.*" (It means: "May your name be inscribed for another good year.") He seemed slightly impressed, but graciously accepted my blessing, even though it was probably spoken in very poor Southern Hebrew.

I also remember another time when I was going to Oxford right before Christmas to do some shopping for Ole Miss gift items. At the time, Jacob managed a large department store in Oxford, and because I was going to that particular store, and because it was a Friday, I decided to bake him and his family a loaf of challah bread, the traditional bread served in Jewish homes for the Sabbath. I made a large loaf of this fabulous bread, took it to him, and he graciously accepted it. That was all there was to it, just a simple gesture of sincere kindness with no strings attached. But, later he told me that it meant a great deal to him because it reminded him of his childhood days growing up and the special bread being baked and served in their home every Sabbath.

I made these random gestures because God put them in my heart, and for no other reason. I was so thankful to be on this journey, and genuinely appreciative of every opportunity.

Several years after we had been sitting next to Jacob at the games, we found out that for whatever reason, his large group of tailgaters had broken up. We insisted that he join us, and he did. As we were not Oxford residents as was he, it was probably somewhat uncomfortable for him to tailgate with mostly strangers from the Memphis area, but he adjusted quickly. Our group welcomed him with open arms, and I personally loved him being there. I loved having a Jewish person around me who could teach me things not to be learned in any other setting.

Jacob always contributed more than his fair share. He was the type of person who remembered everyone. In late October, he would have a plastic pumpkin filled with candy for all the children that came by. Early mornings, he would bring a thermos of hot coffee for the campus police, along with pastries, just in case they had not had breakfast. Sometimes he cooked and sometimes he just bought readymade things. It did not matter. Whatever it was, it was good and greatly appreciated.

One of Jacob's favorite dishes is shrimp jambalaya. He makes it himself with great pride and loves to have people come into our tent to sample. He is proud of his prowess in the kitchen, and by the way the dish is devoured, others are proud of his accomplishments as well. Of course, I do not eat it, but I certainly never say anything to him about what he cooks, and would never have made it a matter of conversation that I would not eat his dish. There is always such a spread that it really does not matter.

One day several of us were gathered under the tent, busy putting out things and doing our usual fussing over food. Jacob was at one end of the line of tables uncovering a dish, and I was at the other end when one of the ladies came up to me and said, "Diane, why don't you eat pork or shrimp?" Before I could say a word, Jacob spoke up without lifting his head or looking in our direction and said, "She eats kosher for me because I won't." That was definitely a Jewish game changer moment! How did he come up with that? I certainly had not planted that in his head; that came from a much Higher Source than I. However, at that moment I told the Lord that although it was not my original intent, I would indeed eat kosher for Naomi, for Jacob and for anyone else God sent my way.

I knew with absolute certainty that my eating kosher was not just a fluke or a whim; it was the calculated design of an always-working, always-connecting Almighty God who does not need our understanding or our approval to ordain a matter.

Comfort ye, comfort ye my people, saith your God.
Isaiah 40:1.

Prayer: Father, it is such a joy and such a "trip" to be your child! You are filled with surprises, and you delight to drop one in on us at the most unusual and most unexpected of times. Thank you that we can trust your hand because we trust your heart. And thank you for the days of hilarious laughter over some of your amazing ways.

Lord, let us truly enjoy this journey! You promised never to leave us or forsake us, and you tell us not to fear what man can do to us. So let us delight ourselves in you and rejoice in being the children of the Most High God! You are our all in all! You make the trip possible, you make the trip eventful and you make the trip successful. In the blessed and dear Name of Jesus I pray, Amen.

11.

The Pardon

My dear Hebrew instructor, Naomi, and I were fast becoming more than teacher and student; we were moving into that deep and abiding bond rarely experienced in life – a friend who sticks closer than a brother. I loved how comfortable I felt with her and how appreciative I was of my having this coveted link with the Jewish world and the vast wealth of knowledge contained therein.

She and I were in contact with each other in some way most every day. I cannot imagine having gone through this life without this incomparable experience. With this friendship came an intimacy that only true friends know and understand. This caliber of friend is one in whom you can confide the most painful, gut-wrenching experiences and know that they will never be served up as gossip, but, rather, will become a shared burden and a continued melding of lives. One friend's secrets rest guarded in the bosom of the other; that was the level of our friendship.

One day when we were together, I began telling Naomi one of the most private, painful chapters of my life. It was a time when one of our sons had gotten into trouble and had been arrested and charged, had to serve probation, and was forever saddled with a felony. It is one of a parent's worst nightmares, and, ours seemed to Ken and me particularly horrendous. As I shared a little of the story with her, she pressed me to tell her everything. As torturous as it was, I relived the whole thing all over again, with no interruptions on her part, and my expectation at story's end of great sympathy and a level of comfort still lacking for this mother.

Our son had been the subject of a sting operation targeting teenagers in a suburb of Memphis with mostly upper class residents. He and one of his best friends had been approached by two very pretty and persuasive, young, undercover officers to buy drugs for them. Our son and his friend told them they only knew where to get marijuana but nothing stronger. The two flirty, vivacious young ladies were very persistent. On at least one occasion, the officers even smoked marijuana with them.

At the police officers' insistence, and being unsuccessful with soliciting anything stronger, the purchase was made for the specified weight of marijuana desired, which in turn was sold to the undercover officers at no profit. Shortly afterward, the police showed up at my son's place of employment, handcuffed and arrested him. A newspaper reporter conveniently was on the scene to capture the whole thing before our son was whisked downtown and booked.

My husband had always told our three sons that if they ever got into trouble with the police that they need not call him. Of course, that was a parental scare tactic; he never really meant it. But, our son must have taken him literally because he did not call us for three days. He was living on his own at the time in an apartment shared with his friend (who was also arrested and promptly bailed out). We kept calling for him, and his friend kept giving us the runaround. We knew something was wrong, but would never have suspected anything like that. Finally, our son called to say that he was in jail, and his Dad, of course, immediately went downtown and bailed him out. Next followed the grueling task of finding a lawyer, the hearings, the pain and the embarrassment, and, to add insult to injury, a multiple-part, carefully planned series began appearing in the local newspaper about teens and drugs in our upscale, sleepy little community. The article on our son carried with it a very large photograph of him bent over a squad car being handcuffed with eyes dead on in the camera. He was devastated, as were we for him. At times, Ken and I truly feared he might do something drastic. That picture alone made us feel as though our family bore the brunt of all of those feature articles.

For the next couple of years, Ken and I had only one life, and it was our son. We went to Sunday School and Church on Sunday mornings, and Ken, of course, went to his job every day, but that was just about the extent of our outside activities. Our constant concern was nurturing and trying to restore to this dear son his dignity and self worth and whatever self-confidence could be regained.

It was all of this, and probably much more, that I poured out to Naomi. I held nothing back. I told her every painful, agonizing detail. When I finished, I looked at her expecting the much-anticipated compassion, but surprisingly received none. Much to my absolute shock, her only response was: "Go get a pardon." Put yourself in my shoes. You have just bared your soul, spilled your insides to your dearest friend, and in return you get this matter-of-fact, out-of-the-blue, off-the-chart response of, "Go get a pardon." Where did that come from? Had she lost her mind?

With my head still reeling, I looked at her and said, "What?" She said, "You heard me; I said go get a pardon." I replied, "I can't do that." (Wrong answer.) She got a little miffed with me and said, "Why not?" (Now *I* was beginning to get miffed.) I said, "Because I don't know how to do that and don't know if I can do that; I don't know anything about all of that." (Wrong answer again.)

Naomi is a lawyer by profession, and although she has not practiced law since coming to America from Israel, I have complete confidence that she was probably quite effective and very forceful when in her official role there. But, this was America and that was Israel. How could she possibly know the process here?

I told her I did not know where to begin or what it entailed; I knew absolutely nothing about pardons. The conversation was something like an incensed mother (her) trying to get through to a stubborn four-year old (me). Frustrated with the whole thing, she finally and firmly told me to call the Governor's office and ask for the forms. By this time I had seen many amazing things God had done with this unique Jewish-Christian oddity, and I also knew that this very well might be one of those times. Not wanting to miss out on any God-sized opportunity, I knew I had to do what she said, mentally calculating that with her by my side (my own built-in lawyer), I had it made. This was going to be a breeze.

I spoke with our son about my pursuing a pardon for him, received his approval and then did exactly as Naomi said. I phoned the Governor's office and asked for the forms. The conversation went something like this: "Hello, my name is Diane McNeil, and I would like to request pardon forms, please." The lady on the other end, after giving a sinister little chuckle, said, "Did you know the Governor receives three hundred pardon requests a year and only grants two?" Of course, I did not know that; how would I know such a thing? Those odds did not sound very good, though, but Naomi told me to do it, and I was doing it. I know the lady thought that after her revelation I would just apologize and go away, but I was on a possible God mission here, and I was not about to be deterred. I said, "Please send me the forms anyway." A little peeved she grudgingly took down my information, and the forms soon arrived in the mail.

I was beginning to get excited about the possibilities of a pardon, and as soon as the forms arrived, I hurried over to Naomi's house to show them off and to see what *we* needed to do next. I flashed them before her face like that same little four-year old, and much to my dismay, she did not seem the least bit interested. She had another home fire to put out at the time. She glanced briefly at the forms, and then told me to get started. I could not believe my ears. Did she really expect me to do all of this by myself? My whole countenance fell. I told her that I did not have the slightest idea where to begin, and her reply was simply, "You'll figure it out." This was not how I had envisioned this playing out.

Extremely dejected, I left with forms in hand, wondering what on earth I had gotten myself into. And, let me give you a little heads up, these were not "yes" and "no" answers, but, rather, extensive, fact finding research. If not for what I had already seen God do with unified Jews and Christians, I would have probably gone home and put the forms in a drawer somewhere and moved on with my life – but God . . .

I began my dark journey – alone. Even Ken told me I was wasting my time. He said that the Governor would never grant this pardon because it would not look good for the powers that be. But I had no choice. I did not have a word from the Lord on this, just an inner knowing that God was in the midst of it.

I did bounce things off Naomi at times, but for the most part she maintained her stand that I would figure it out. It took nearly a year for the book of information to be collected and catalogued in the manner that I felt was acceptable and thorough – a year filled with visits to another lawyer friend; conversations with police officers about the incident; trips to the newspaper reporter's office (the one who conveniently happened to be on the scene to capture our son's arrest); hours of writing and research and gathering; and then, to the best of my ability, formatting it. It was finally complete. But, throughout this ordeal, the words of the lady I spoke with in the Governor's office kept ringing in my ear: "He receives three hundred requests a year and only grants two." I wondered if that were really true.

I mailed the completed packet of material and waited. Sometime later, we received notice that there was going to be a hearing with the Board of Pardons, and our son and his new wife were to be present. Ken and I were permitted to attend as well. He and I sat in the back of the room listening to every word. We were only addressed a couple of times. I thought our son handled himself quite well, and thought the hearing went in his favor. I did not know if that meant anything, but that was how it appeared to me. At the end of the meeting, they took a poll of all of the officials on the Board present as to whether or not to recommend a pardon to the Governor, and they each voted affirmatively. I thought that was definitely encouraging, so, we all left with high hopes.

However, a great deal of time passed, and we heard nothing further. I was so afraid this matter had fallen between the cracks somewhere and that we had been overlooked. Not only that, but the Governor's maximum two terms were about to come to an end, and we needed this to be finalized before he left office. The next Governor very well might not be so inclined to grant even two pardons a year (if that really was true). I was getting that same sickening feeling in the pit of my stomach all over again, a feeling I know all too well, and I guess Naomi was tired of listening to me, because she told me to call the Governor's office and see what I could find out. So I did.

I think I got that same lady again. I told her I was calling to check on the progress of our son's pardon appeal. It seemed I was bothering her again, and she said, "Well, what was the vote at the Pardons Hearing?" I told her they all voted in favor of recommending a pardon for our son. Her whole demeanor changed, and she said, "They *all* voted in favor?" I assured her they did, and she said, "That never happens." She looked up our son's case and said that it was on the list for the Governor to consider. ("Thank you, Lord.") I hung up the phone, greatly relieved that it was still moving forward.

Before the Governor left office, we received that anticipated letter, signed by the Governor of the Great State of Tennessee, granting our son an executive pardon. Although it has long since been filed away, it will forever be framed on the walls of my heart. What a journey; what a success story, and all because of my precious Jewish friend saying, "Go get a pardon." If I had a thousand lifetimes to live, it would not be enough to adequately thank her for making me think outside my little box. What a friend! What a Jewish game changer!

Let me share something incredible that we learned along the way. An executive pardon means that legally the crime never occurred. It removes every aspect of the wrongdoing. It does not just make it right; it makes it non-existent. "In the United States . . . the Supreme Court has held that a pardon blots out guilt and makes the offender 'as innocent as if he had never committed the offense,'" (www.squidoo.com).

This gave me a grateful new appreciation for the pardon we have in Christ Jesus, our Great High Executive who pardons and eradicates for all time and eternity our ever having committed any and all offenses. Astonishing!

One final thing: When I read the newspaper article about our Governor's final days in office, it reported that during his eight-year term, he granted sixteen pardons, two a year, just as the lady had told me – and, Praise God, ours was one of them!

> *For a small moment have I forsaken thee; but with great mercies will I gather thee. In a little wrath I hid my face from thee for a moment; but with everlasting kindness will I have mercy on thee, saith the Lord thy Redeemer.* (Isaiah 54:7-8).

Prayer: Oh, Lord, thank you for who you are! Thank you that you are not some wooden or golden statue sitting on a stand – made by human hands. Thank you that we cannot box you in. Thank you that there are no boundaries with you; there is nothing out of reach for you. You are vast beyond all measure yet, you are ever the personal, intimate God who sees all, knows all and who is personally involved in all. You know when we lie down and when we rise up, and not only do you know it, but you are right there beside us, every step of the way. You are amazing! Oh, the height and depth and breadth of your matchless, boundless love, for which I am eternally thankful. Oh God, I Love You, and I praise you and magnify you! To you be all glory forever and ever! In your sweet Son's Name, I surrender all, Amen.

TENNESSEE
EXECUTIVE CHAMBER

PARDON

TO WHOM THESE PRESENTS SHALL COME, GREETINGS:

WHEREAS, the Constitution and laws of the State of Tennessee grant the Governor the power and authority to grant pardons as he may deem proper,

THEREFORE, I HEREBY, gr⸺ ⸻ Neil a full pardon for his 1990 conviction for possession of a ⸻ ⸻arijuana) with intent to manufacture, deliver, or sell. M⸻ ⸻ a good citizen and shall not violate any of the laws of ⸻ ⸻essee or any other state, municipality or county and sha⸻ ⸻ch is illegal or improper in the opinion of the Governor.

IN TESTIMONY WHEREOF, I have hereunto set my hand and caused the Great Seal of the State to be affixed at Nashville, Tennessee, on the 20th day of December, 2001.

GOVERNOR

Governor's Letter of Pardon

12.

A Christian and the Sabbath

One cannot be involved in Jewish life long before sensing the uniqueness of the Sabbath. It is worlds apart from our Sunday, which is not the Sabbath. I remember as a young girl growing up in a small Mississippi Delta town and hearing my elders speak reverently of Sunday as the Sabbath, and of prayers in our church services thanking God that we could come together and worship on the Sabbath. Sunday is a special day in the life of Christianity; it is the day set apart for our worship, but it has not always been so. The First Century Church worshipped on the Sabbath, as did the Jews. However, during the time of the Emperor Constantine, desiring to distance Christians from Jews, he decreed that the day for the Church to worship would be changed to Sunday and it was and still is so to this day for the majority of Christendom.

I wish every born-again believer could step into that twenty-four hour, hallowed day in Jewish life, even if for just one Shabbat (the term many Jews use when referring to the Sabbath). As best as my words are able to convey, and through some of my experiences, I am going to try and briefly immerse you into that beloved and highly revered seventh day of the week, the Sabbath.

The first time Ken and I observed Shabbat was in preparation for our trip to Israel with members of the little Messianic Jewish Synagogue in Memphis. There were about a dozen of us signed up for that journey of a lifetime and often Ken and I would receive a phone call mid-week inviting us to come to Shabbat dinner to schmooze (a Yiddish word many Jewish people use meaning to meet and greet) in anticipation of our Holy Land trip. Those Friday evenings were like stepping into another time and another place.

The Sabbath is the only day in the Bible that is named. The other days are referenced according to their relationship to the Sabbath: the *first* day of the week (after the Sabbath), the *second*, and so on. The Sabbath begins at sundown Friday and ends at sundown Saturday. In the creation account, God's Word says that the "evening and the morning were the first day," and because God began the days at evening, so do the Jews. You also might find it interesting that this day is also considered a holiday. It is a set-apart day, a holy day, a highly honored day, a greatly anticipated day.

Sabbath means "to cease or rest;" therefore, no work is done. It is a day to worship, enjoy family and catch your breath in the midst of the chaotic frenzy of life. That is how God intended it to be, and that is how vast numbers of Jews celebrate it today.

There is much hustle and bustle on Fridays in preparation for the Sabbath. One friend reminisced about how her mother and aunt used to spend the entire day together cooking while she and the other children played and stayed out of their way. When she talked of those times, a smile would instantly streak across her face, and I could sense her stepping back in time remembering the joy of those special times. That is exactly how God intended it – a day in which to rejoice, a delight to savor. (Sadly, she lost her entire family in the Holocaust.)

In a traditional Jewish home, the mother does the grocery shopping, cleans the house and prepares a festive holiday meal, all by Friday sundown. Oftentimes, and possibly all of the time for many, the best china, silver and linens are brought out, and favorite dishes are prepared. As sundown approaches, the family will arrive home and wash (literally, and in some homes, ritually) for the meal. The Sabbath begins with the woman of the house, head covered, lighting two Shabbat candles, fanning the aroma of the candles into her nostrils (breathing in the fragrance of the special day) and speaking a Hebrew blessing over the set-apart day. (I was told that there are two candles lit because God's Word commanded that they: (1) remember the Sabbath day; and (2) keep it holy.) At that moment, the outside world ceases, and for the next twenty-four hours, the franticness of life is put on hold and God and his day command center stage.

A special bread known as challah is baked for the Shabbat meal, and while it is being broken, another Hebrew blessing is spoken before passing it around for all to enjoy. Next comes the blessing of the fruit of the vine, followed by blessings spoken over members of the family. The father will bless his wife and children, and in some homes, she will respond in like manner. What an incredible experience for children week after week after week – what a lifelong impact this must certainly make!

Families go to synagogue, have friends and extended family over to share in their Shabbat meal, play games together, etc. It is a day to robustly enjoy life; it is God's gift. I once had a Jewish friend to tell me that since it is such a joyful occasion, oftentimes there is intimacy between husband and wife. That shocked me because at the time my mind conjured up mental pictures of everyone walking around all hushed and reverent – something like monks. I was completely off base; it is a much-anticipated, robust, delightful holiday occurring each week.

I love bread making, and when we first started going to the Messianic Jewish homes for Shabbat dinners, I was immediately interested in trying my hand at baking the challah for our next gathering, realizing that in many Jewish homes where kosher is strictly observed, food prepared in a non-kosher kitchen (Gentile at that) would never be allowed. Thankfully, that was not the case in these homes. They gratefully accepted my offer. I found a recipe and have been baking it ever since. I cherished those Friday evenings and my presenting the woman of the house with my freshly-baked loaf of challah. It was as though we were allowed to share in this day with them, and I loved the feeling of having a part.

I soon became quite good at baking challah and found myself wanting to make two loaves every Friday, one for our family and one to share with whatever Jewish friend God brought to mind (if their religious beliefs allowed). I can remember one Friday afternoon going to the home of a dear Jewish lady I had come to know and love. (She is the Holocaust survivor I mentioned in the first part of this chapter.) We first met when I attended several functions at which she was speaking about her Holocaust experiences. Over time, a unique bond formed between us, and I wanted to favor her with the fruits of my labor.

I arrived at her home late afternoon that particular Friday and knocked at the door proudly bearing my Shabbat offering. She greeted me, all smiles, wearing her flour-dusted apron. She seemed delighted with the challah. We stood on the doorstep and chatted for a few minutes, and I soon found myself mesmerized by her twinkling eyes. They seemed to be dancing all over her face. Everything about her looked as if she were a little girl about to burst with excitement. I had never seen her like that before, and could not help but comment. I said, "You look as though you are excited about something." A smile spread from ear to ear, and she replied, "I am." Then, she walked a few steps to the carport and peered around the corner up into the western sky and the setting sun and said, "Look, it is almost the Sabbath." I must confess, at that moment my whole countenance fell and a strange sensation of jealousy swept over me. Why was it that she had this personal connection with God's set-apart day and I did not? In that moment I actually felt as though I had been spiritually robbed of something, and I did not like that feeling one bit. How could she know and love this day so passionately, while I, a born-again, Bible-loving, fervent-in-prayer Christian had zero understanding?

All the way home and for many days afterward, I was haunted by her enthusiasm and passion for the Sabbath. She was drenched with delight over that coming day! I want everything God has for me, and I have told the Lord that many, many times. I found myself wondering if it were possible for Christians to observe the Sabbath when our day of worship is on Sunday. Could we enter into this day of rest, this day of bliss, or was it for Jews only? How much of it, if any, could I bring into our home? Was I crazy to be having these thoughts? Was Ken going to think I had finally gone off the deep end? Maybe I could just do it and not tell him what was going on. Oh, the thoughts that ran though my head! But, I could not let it go – or rather, it would not let me go.

I soon found myself on my own Sabbath quest to see if there was any connection there for me, the Christian, and God's appointed day, the Sabbath. I prayed about it and told the Lord that as best as I knew how, I was going on my own fact-finding mission to see if I could discover the same love of the day that my Jewish friend had. My plan was to get all of my housework completed, the grocery shopping done, the meal prepared, and then between sundown Friday and sundown Saturday do nothing that in my mind translated work. I asked the Lord to show me personally – Diane McNeil – if there was anything there for me as a Christian.

It was actually a lot easier than I dreamed possible. I loved the fact that for one whole day I did nothing that I considered to be work: no ironing, no cleaning bathrooms, no laundry, no scrubbing floors, etc. If Ken was working in the yard, I might piddle in my flowers to be near him, but, for me, that is not work, that is fun. I kind of liked this new routine. I liked having the twenty-four hour no-work zone, but I was not content with that – I wanted to see God in it – personally. I wanted to know what He thought of my new routine, or whether or not He even cared.

One Friday afternoon, well into my experiment – with the house cleaned and the shopping done – the phone rang. It was a dear Messianic Jewish friend who was calling to ask for prayer for another close Jewish friend whose father was at the point of death. I was asked to pray for the beloved Jewish father and for all the family. Then, to further compound the situation, I was told that this particular friend had promised her home to another Messianic Jewish family whose daughter was having her bat-mitzvah that weekend and needed a place to host the Shabbat meal. However, now that her father was near death, she could no longer open her home for this joyous celebration.

My head was spinning; I knew all of these people and loved each one of them dearly. What a terrible dilemma for all involved. The bat mitzvah family had friends and family coming in from out of state, and what were they going to do last minute? My heart was breaking for them. Then I said to the caller, "My house is clean, and I would be honored to offer our home for this special Shabbat dinner, if it would be appropriate." A few phone calls later, and the arrangements were made. This *Jewish* family was coming into our *Gentile* home, bringing the already prepared dishes to celebrate bat mitzvah for their young daughter. I put out my best linens, china, crystal and silver. Ken came in from work and was shocked to find that we were going out for dinner and would not be able to return for several hours. And, although he was, to say the least, a little caught off-guard by the matter, he, too, was more than happy to accommodate.

Do you see the miraculous in what took place? Never, ever would that or could that have happened if I had not been on my own spiritual pursuit of understanding what connection the Sabbath might possibly hold for this Gentile Christian. My genuine (albeit probably quite naïve) obedience opened the door for God to do something so large that even now I stagger at its ramifications. I, by faith, had put myself in a position for God to show me personally His heart for the Sabbath, and I found that his heart has not changed since Exodus 31:16 where he said, *"Wherefore the children of Israel shall keep the Sabbath, to observe the Sabbath throughout their generations, for a perpetual covenant."* Yes, it does say that it is for the children of Israel, but what I have come to understand is that God graciously allows the alien and the stranger to come into this privileged position as well, if he or she so desires. It is certainly not mandatory for the Christian, as it is for the Jews, but it is not off-limits either. He is a loving God who wants all His children to experience His fullness. This was one Jewish game changer I will never forget and will cherish for as long as I live.

The mother of the bat mitzvah daughter told me some time later that her family was stunned that a Christian would care enough to open their home to Jews. It was astonishing to all her non-believing family. We will never know this side of Heaven the sum total of God-things unleashed in the spiritual realm when we dare to step out in faith and do those things prompted by God, though possibly foreign to us.

Pray for the peace of Jerusalem: they shall prosper that love thee. Psalm 122:6.

Prayer: Oh, Lord, I do love Israel and the Jews. I know your heart for her; you have revealed it to me time and time again. She is the wife of your choosing, and your eye is ever watchful over her. No weapon formed against her will ever prosper. Oh, Lord, may the Church be your and her greatest cheerleader! May we be voices that will not be silenced, always in support of your Chosen. May we come alongside her and unwaveringly take our stand. May we be her constant companion, and may our avowed support for her rise up as a sweet-smelling aroma to your holy throne. We delight to be used of you, Lord, in this choicest of all fields. In the sweet Name of Jesus I pray, Amen.

CHALLAH
JEWISH BRAIDED BREAD

½ C. plus 2 T. Warm Water
1 Envelope Yeast (2-1/4 t.)
1 T. plus 1-1/2 t. Sugar
¼ C. plus 2 T. Vegetable Oil
2-3/4 – 3 C. Unbleached Plain Flour
2 Eggs at Room Temperature
1-1/2 t. Salt
2-4 t. Sesame Seeds
1 Egg Beaten with Pinch of Salt for Glaze

In a small bowl or two-cup measure, combine yeast with ¼ C. warm water; add 1 t. sugar; let proof for 15 minutes. In large bowl, sift flour and salt together and make well in middle. Add yeast and remaining ingredients, except seeds and egg for glaze. Stir with wooden spoon. Turn out on floured surface and knead 7 minutes. Oil bowl and place dough in it, turning to coat with oil. Cover loosely with cellophane stretch wrap sprayed with cooking spray and let rise 1-1/4 hours. Turn out on floured surface again and knead. Return to bowl and allow to rise for 1 hour, loosely covered. Divide dough into thirds and shape each into a ball. Cover and let rest 10 minutes on counter so dough is easier to handle. On a lightly floured surface, roll each ball into an even, thick rope about 16 inches long. Line up the three ropes, 1 inch apart, on a greased baking sheet.

Beginning in the middle of the ropes and working toward the ends, braid loosely, pinch ends together and tuck under the braid. Cover loosely and let rise 1 hour until almost doubled. Brush with beaten egg and salt mixture and sprinkle with seeds. Bake approximately 35-40 minutes at 350 degrees. This makes 1 braided loaf.

(Often the recipe is doubled for a large loaf for the Sabbath since the children of Israel were told to gather a double portion of manna before the Sabbath.)

13.

The Remembering

Shortly before Christian Friends of Israel – Memphis officially presented our Jewish community with their Israeli Red Cross ambulance, God gave our committee a new assignment. The ambulance had just arrived and was parked at the entrance of the Jewish Community Center to proudly display. Several of us from the committee were excitedly watching as the Jewish people checked out their ambulance, usually in a somewhat confused state because of the inscription on the front door that said it was a gift from Christians. Donna, one of the committee members, pulled me aside and said she needed to talk to me.

The two of us retreated to my car, and before she could tell me what was on her mind, tears began to flow. She said, "I believe God is telling me that we need to do something for Yom HaShoah." (I did not have the slightest idea what that was – she had to explain that it is Hebrew for Holocaust Memorial Day.) "Well, when is it," I asked. "Next month," she said. I knew there was absolutely no way we could pull anything off on such short notice. We had not even finalized everything with the ambulance. But, I also knew it was from the Lord, and said, "Donna, we can't do anything this year, but let's see where God will take this next year." We prayed together and were excited to share our new direction with the rest of the committee.

After the ambulance was presented to our local Jewish community at their celebration honoring Israel's fiftieth birthday as a nation and then being delivered to Israel, we took some time off to catch our collective breaths. The first campaign had been so exciting and so successful, and we were eager to see what God had in store for project number two. We held our first meeting to talk about Yom HaShoah – Hebrew for day of destruction – Holocaust Memorial Day. We had no idea what was in store, but what we did know was that God was in it and we had a specific timeframe in which to work because it is a set date on the calendar.

Once again we started up our weekly meetings, and it was incredible to see how things began to unfold. Mary Jane remembered seeing a riveting piece of Holocaust art at a Jewish Community Center in Youngstown, Ohio, and volunteered to check that out. Others wanted local Holocaust survivors to share their stories – possibly on video. Another found the book, *I Never Saw Another Butterfly*, and wanted to incorporate that into our project. The consensus of the committee was that we should pay tribute to the 1,500,000 children who perished in the Holocaust. That became our focus: telling the story of the children.

Over the ensuing months, we had one victory after another as we pursued this next walk of faith. Each committee member found his or her own niche and honed in on it. What we saw coming to life was our hosting a Holocaust Exhibit for the entire month of April (1999), the month Yom HaShoah is observed. We did not deviate from our initial strategy of running all things considered past the heads of the Memphis Jewish Federation and nixing those that did not meet with their approval – no questions asked. And, yes, there were times we were stopped in our tracks and had to alter our course, but even in those times, the new route taken proved better than the original.

One such alteration was the time we heard about a video featuring local Holocaust survivors' testimonies which we wanted to present in the opening part of the exhibit. We called around and located a copy and were thrilled. That is, until we received a call from an irate Jewish man who had suffered in the Holocaust. He gave me quite a tongue-lashing for proposing to use something that was copyrighted, and on and on. I quickly apologized and told him we would not use the video. As soon as I hung up, I phoned another Holocaust survivor and explained our dilemma and asked if there was anything else out there we could use. She was incensed that we were refused the use of that video and told me that she would contact two other Holocaust survivors, and if we could arrange for the taping, they would make a video just for us. We found an absolutely amazing company, whose owner had such a tender heart toward the Jewish people and the Holocaust that he agreed to donate his services. We ended up with our very own video of three amazing survivors and their impassioned, unimaginable remembrances. One survivor was nine at the time of his capture, one was twelve, and the other about fifteen, just children – our focus. (Thank you, God, for your favor and for this amazing Jewish game changer.)

Mary Jane did, indeed, locate Frank Root, the artist whose relief she had seen in Youngstown. Frank lives in the Philadelphia area and is an incredibly gifted artist with an amazing story about his personal connection with the Holocaust. His work has been commissioned by the likes of Frank Sinatra and other notables. Frank Root is also a musician, and he shared with us that one night while performing, he had a heart attack and died. He said that while he was out of his body, the Lord spoke to him and said that he was not going to die, but when he came back, he must create Holocaust art, an entirely new venue for him. He was revived and knew without a doubt that his career had taken on a new God-sized direction.

Frank Root's is one of the most creative minds on and off the canvas. His Holocaust art is captured in 3-D reliefs that compel and draw the viewer into his mastermind world. His work is gripping, heart-wrenching, commanding – far beyond anything I can relate. Not only did Mary Jane find him, but she found him interested in our project and willing to work with us.

One of the most thrilling things that happened for us was our finding a place to house our little exhibit, which, ironically, was named by our now new Jewish friend (the one who had refused to allow us to use the existing video of the local survivors' testimonies). He said we should call it *The Remembering*, and we did. Kirby Woods Baptist Church, where several on the committee were members, was in the midst of a building program, and the church had a wing that would soon be torn down. This wing had been the original sanctuary and then later became the nursery, with some eight rooms, restrooms, the required fire exits; it had everything! This part of the church was now empty, awaiting demolition, and they offered it to us for the month of the scheduled exhibit. It was ours to do with as we pleased, and it was a good thing because Frank Root required that his art be displayed on black walls with overhead canned lighting. That church had never before seen black rooms, and certainly not in their former nursery. We did not have to pay utilities or get permission for anything; it was an amazing Godsend! Not only that, but its location is on the busiest, most visible street in the City of Memphis, about a quarter of a mile from the Jewish Community Center. When God does something, He does it exceptionally well!

The finished product was far beyond anything any of us could ever have imagined. And, remember, the people on this committee are not influential, wealthy or part of the Memphis elite. We are the average God-fearing folks that you might ask to help change a tire or watch your children while you go to the doctor. We were commoners whom God used on a very uncommon assignment.

When the last paint can was sealed, the lights all hung, the floors swept, the final inspection by the Memphis Jewish Federation and the "Open for Business" sign hung, we had a first-class Children's Holocaust Exhibit. In the entry there were loaned benches for seating, a welcome station manned by volunteer greeters handing out booklets for the visitor to use on the self-guided tour. There was a hushed reverence at all times, without prompting. Yet, there was one constant sound: a bell tolling at two-second intervals for the duration of the month-long exhibit – 1,500,000 tolls – the number of children killed during the Holocaust.

The visitor was directed into the first room where our continuous-feed video of the survivors' testimonies played on a huge donated television screen. Following that were four black painted rooms displaying Frank Root's artwork. His Holocaust reliefs tell the full story: the early dark days, Kristallnacht (the night the Germans destroyed most all of the synagogues in Germany and parts of Austria), the trains, the concentration camps, the Auschwitz killing wall, the ovens, etc.

Following the art display was a room where we had reenacted a playground, similar to the ones set up by the Nazis for the purpose of capturing innocent children who went there to play while their parents were on forced labor assignments. All the contents in this room were donated, along with a smoke machine that cast an eerie pall over the entire setting.

Next came a room showcasing the artwork of the children of the Terezenstadt concentration camp, as featured in the book *I Never Saw Another Butterfly*. In that camp, a compassionate woman gave the children art classes to divert, at least for a brief moment, their attention from the many being tortured and murdered daily. In this area there were also two large viewing windows (originally used for looking into the nursery rooms). In one we showcased loaned Holocaust memorabilia. There were diaries and photos of family members taken before their deaths in the camps, period newspapers, Nazi helmets and badges. Behind the other we staged a mock barracks similar to those in the death camps. Jon, a committee member, built wooden cubicles for sleeping in which straw was sparsely placed. In the barracks area was also a small pot-bellied stove, bowls for whatever watered-down gruel they were fed and a few other grim items.

Following that was the map room where Janie (our own in-house professional mapmaker) had scaled a map of Europe on a 12-foot-by-12-foot canvas cloth, and which highlighted all the many camps. Also in this room were displayed loaned, original black and white photos of life in that part of the world at the beginning of the Holocaust.

The final room had a story all its own. In our early planning stages, one of the things that kept surfacing was our wanting a "lights and mirrors" display similar to the Spiegel Memorial in Jerusalem. As only a couple on the committee had actually seen this memorial, it was hard to relay to the others how to capture its uniqueness. The Spiegel Memorial is a one-room phenomenon. As you enter the structure, you are instantly struck by name after name being called out over the loud speaker. You walk farther into the room and notice that there are seven candles strategically placed, surrounded by mirrors which multiply the seven lights into millions. The names you hear over the speakers are those who were killed in the Holocaust. It is one of the most haunting memorials imaginable, and we wanted somehow to recreate this in our exhibit. The problem was that if you had never seen it, you could not grasp the concept, and Jon had not seen it at the time.

Jon tinkered and tinkered, trying to replicate what we were describing to him, but it was not working. Then the time came to travel to Philadelphia to pick up Frank Root's reliefs. When we entered Frank's and Ruth's home, I immediately noticed sitting over in the corner of their living room a small replica of the lights and mirrors exhibit that Frank had built. There it stood right before our very eyes! If there were ever any doubts up to this point as to whether or not this exhibit was really God's assignment, they vanished in that moment. Jon was standing right there seeing with his own eyes what we had been trying to describe. Not only did he view this re-creation, but Frank told him exactly how to construct it to achieve the desired results. It was one of those indescribable moments when God's presence was everywhere. Truly, everything about The Remembering was an incredible game changer.

We had our grand opening event with Frank Root as special guest. There were as many Jewish people in attendance as Christians. We knew without a doubt that God was smiling down on our little opening night celebration and the unity it produced between Jews and Christians.

During the month-long exhibit, some 5,000 visitors passed through, including all area Jewish schools and several public and private school groups. We did not charge admission, but we did accept donations. At the final tally, we had enough money (including some leftover funds from the ambulance) to pay passage for seventy Russian Jews to make aliyah (move) to Israel.

Oh, how our hearts thrilled with the tremendous success of that assignment! But, somehow we all knew that far more had been accomplished in God's Kingdom than was visible on the surface. Truly, we felt that God was well pleased with our efforts.

> *And I will bless them that bless thee* (Israel), *and curse him that curseth thee, and in thee shall all families of the earth be blessed.* Genesis 12:3.

Prayer: Father, I love this exciting journey. It does have its ups and downs, but you are right there with us through every one of them. You rise and fall alongside us; you never leave us or forsake us. And, these ups and downs are not to harm or to discourage us, but to strengthen us and to bring glory to yourself! Thank you, Lord, for the success of The Remembering and for the lives that were changed, but there is so much more work yet to be done. Lord, let our blessing Israel produce a desire in others to bless her, too, and may this zeal for Zion permeate all the true Church throughout the world. May we all want a part in this God-blessed assignment. Give each of us our own unique, personal tasks, and may we not rest until our mission is accomplished – for your Name's sake! Lord, we are so in love with you. In the Name of Jesus, Amen.

The Remembering Picture

14.

The Book Goes to the Publisher

In the second chapter, I told of my Ruth encounter, which sent me on my first-ever writing assignment. One of the most difficult, yet one of the most rewarding, challenges of my life was writing *Ruth 3,000 years of Sleeping Prophecy Awakened*. It was ten years of being in a constant quandary over whether or not I was really supposed to be doing such a thing – writing a Bible study? I was anything but a Bible scholar. Of course, I loved the Bible; I read it every day, but that is a far cry from someone who is a student of the Word and who studies under brighter minds than their own.

Let me tell you why I read my Bible every day. When I was fourteen, I did something incredibly stupid. I do not recall what it was, which is probably a good thing but whatever it was, I told the Lord if He would get me out of that mess I would read my Bible every day for the rest of my life. That has been fifty years ago, and except for a couple of misses, I have kept my promise. However, that hardly qualifies me to write what I consider to be a major, prophetic, in-depth study from the Word of God.

What does qualify me, though, is that God distinctly called me to the task, and I faithfully stayed the course until it was completed (1995-2005). Were there ups and downs and mountains and valleys and starts and stops along the way? You bet there were. At times it was such a painful struggle. Ken would say to me, "Honey, you're never going to finish that book," and I would laugh (on the outside) and assure him that I would finish some day. Yet, deep down I had my own sphere of doubts, and it always came down to one thing: "Who am *I* to write a Bible study?"

Oh, how my inadequacy pained me; nonetheless, I trudged on always imploring God for the book's every need. My ten-year assignment was nearing completion, and the book was almost finished. As a matter of fact, I recall that I had announced to Ken that I was taking the coming weekend for myself, and then the book would be finished! I was so close that I could taste it. There were only a few final things that needed to be shored up, and as that particular weekend approached, I was ecstatic with the thoughts of finally bringing to a close this enormous undertaking.

Weekend was coming and I had only one thing on my mind: finishing the book, but God, it seemed, had other plans. Early one morning the phone rang, and it was one of my oldest and dearest friends. I answered and Beverly's ever-cheerful voice immediately chimed in with the purpose for the call: she and Bob wanted to come for the weekend. Oh, how my heart sank! Ken and I both love their visits. We had been friends for over twenty-five years. We had watched each other's children grow up and knew almost as much about each of them as we did our own. "Any weekend, Beverly – just not this one!" That was what I wanted to say, but, of course, friends do not say that to friends. I replied, "Absolutely!" with a smile on the outside and moans on the inside. I was beside myself! This was not a part of my plan.

Friday came, and I had a special dinner prepared. There was a lot of laughter. We thoroughly enjoy each other's company (well, I tried to enjoy it). Afterward, we played our usual round of dominos. The guys had tee times for golf the next day, and I had decided to take Beverly to a small neighboring town that had a quaint town square lined with restaurants and unique shops. The next day arrived and she and I headed out on our excursion. We had lunch and wandered in and out of the shops, something I would normally enjoy – but just not this weekend!

We went into one of the charming antique shops and Beverly took off in one direction and I in another, just wanting to be alone to try and process why God was not giving me my weekend to finish the book. As I walked toward the back of the store, I found myself praying a prayer that I had prayed probably a hundred times during the course of this ten-year writing process. I said, "Lord, if this really is your book, and if you really have called me to do this, then, please give me something – personally from you to me – to let me know (again) that I really am about my Father's business."

I continued milling around, looking at things with which I had grown up and marveling that they are now called antiques. As I reached the back room, I glanced up, and hanging on the back wall was a very old, wood-carved, oval picture frame with period bowed-out glass encasing a picture with several holes in it because of its age. I looked at the tag on it and it read, "Bible characters – $65." While I surmised that it was probably not worth $65, it was worth a million to me. It was the new cover for my book – an incredible picture of Naomi and Ruth! That was my picture! That was my personal gift from God, and it was His way of saying again, for the hundredth time, that I really was supposed to be writing this book. It truly was my assignment. I stood, spellbound, gazing at the treasure, then took it off the wall and hurried to find Beverly. I showed her the picture and told her it was going to be the new cover for my book, and she was almost as shocked as I was. We both knew that being in that place and discovering that treasure was a divine appointment.

(When the time came for me to send my proposal for the cover to the publisher, I removed my "holey" picture from the frame and took it to a local print shop. I paid $5 to have a color copy made, and sent it to the publisher. They were able to shade in the holes and interject new life into the faded color, resulting in an amazing cover for a very special book. "Thank you again Lord!")

Needless to say, I had to repent for not embracing God's change in plans that weekend. When will I ever get it that His ways really are higher than mine? And, when will I ever *Trust in the Lord with all my heart and <u>lean not to my own understanding</u>; in all my ways acknowledge Him and* [allow Him to] *direct my path*?

However, there were still hurdles that were yet to fall in place in this incredible puzzle. One was the cost of publishing. I had sent the manuscript to several main-stream Christian publishers, only to receive the standard rejection letters. In researching the process, I came to understand that for a publisher to take a manuscript, turn it into a book and promote it costs something like $50,000. For that very legitimate reason, most publishers shy away from first-time writers. I dejectedly came to the realization that if I wanted this book in print, I had to self-publish.

I had no idea whatsoever how or where to begin the process of looking for a publisher until one day when a dear friend appeared at my back door holding a small piece of paper she had torn from a magazine. She had seen this advertisement in World Magazine (a reputable source) for a Christian self-publishing company and she thought I should check it out. I went on-line to research this publisher, and was pleasantly surprised and impressed. As a matter of fact, I felt that this was a God-send. But there was one slight, little glitch: publishing costs plus a generous supply of books would run around $2,500, something I absolutely did not have.

A short time later, as I was sitting in front of the computer, peering at the manuscript on the screen, I prayed and asked the Lord to send the money. I knew if I had gone to Ken and asked for it, he would have found a way, but I really did not want to do that to him. One of our sons had been in some serious legal battles, and Ken had gone way out on a limb for him. I was not about to add more pressure on an already drained and dry precious man. So, I went to a far greater Source, One who loves me even more than Ken does. I did not tell anyone about praying for that money; I just left it in the bosom of my Heavenly Father.

About a year before that, the same friend that had brought me the article from World Magazine told me that she was moving from the house where she had been born and had lived all her eighty years. Her immediate family was gone, and I knew she could probably use some help. I also knew that because of our son and his ominous legal battles, this would be a welcome diversion for me – something to take my mind off my own weight of woes. So I volunteered my help and she gladly accepted. For the next several weeks and months, she and I were together almost every week day. We cleaned out, weeded out, routed out, threw out, shredded, on and on and on throughout this wonderful place she had always called home. It was a very rewarding challenge; actually, I thoroughly enjoyed it. We never knew what surprising discoveries each new day might bring, and there were a few. But, I was also very mindful that this represented many precious years and many lives that I was sifting through, and I tried with everything in me to be extremely respectful of that. It was her whole lifetime packed into that home; it was her journey, and I wanted to handle it with utmost care.

We made it through the move with each of us intact and still great friends. She settled into an independent living facility where she has adapted quite well. I was grateful to have been a part of her journey and grateful for the diversion.

I never thought anything about my helping her, but she did. Some time later, after she was situated in her new place and had her affairs in order, she called and said she needed to see me. We met halfway in the parking lot of a local hardware store. I got into the front seat of her car, we chatted a little while, and then she handed me a card. I was somewhat confused because it was not a special occasion; yet, I knew by the look on her face that it was more than that. I opened it and a check fell out. I read the thank you note and unfolded the check. It was made payable to me in the amount of $2,500. "I can't take this – but I have to – I prayed for this," I said. It was bittersweet; I did not want to take her money, but I had asked God for this money; I had no recourse. God sent my publishing money through my friend's exceptional generosity. He answered my prayer! It really was His book. I will never get over the lavishness of His faithfulness in every circumstance, no matter what it looked like at the time. Praise His Holy Name!

So, I had the publisher and the money, but there was one remaining obstacle – endorsements. I was a female with absolutely no credentials (by the world's standards), so I felt I had to have prominent male figures to write endorsements – to validate this book and me. I decided to approach three men I knew personally, each of whom had a measure of clout. One was our pastor, who was highly respected in religious circles; another was a pastor from Florida who had a large church with an affiliated Bible college; and the third was a prominent man in our community who worked diligently promoting Jewish-Christian relations, and many years back had run for President of the United States. These would make three very good endorsements, and I had all the confidence in the world that I would receive all three. I composed my letters, enclosed copies of the manuscript, hand-delivered one and mailed the other two, then waited expectantly. I received no response from one; the second sent a glowing endorsement and then shortly afterward was fired from his position; and the third sent an equally good endorsement and then died soon thereafter. How could that have happened? What was I to do now?

I sat there looking at the manuscript on the computer screen, and I said to the Lord, probably with a bit of an attitude, "I am mailing this tomorrow, and I have no endorsements, so I guess you don't want this book to have any." (He and I have had many such conversations.) A short time later, I opened my e-mails, and what awaited me was my endorsement, right before my very eyes and right on time. It had come not as I had anticipated, but exactly as God had designed. This was from a young Hispanic woman (so much for the fact that I thought it had to be a male figurehead). She was writing about the weekend she and I met at an Eagles Retreat Bible study and prayer group. On our final day together, I had been asked to share from my study of Ruth, which I was thrilled to do. This young lady was writing me about that teaching. Below is her letter (the endorsement):

I wanted to tell you what God has done in my life since the Eagles weekend getaway, hosted by our dear friend Debra.

On Sunday morning you shared with us from your study on the Book of Ruth. It was so powerful that it's changed my life. A love for Israel was birthed in my heart and in my spirit for God's Nation. The passion with which you shared about Israel has forever forged a passion in my own life for this great Nation. I knew when I left Reelfoot Lake, Tennessee, that I was changed. I came home and found myself being awakened in the night with a burden and a love for Israel that wasn't there until that weekend. I found myself weeping for this wonderful Nation. And, it didn't just happen one night, it was often. I told Debra, "Diane has 'messed me up.' I find myself weeping for the Nation of Israel, and I find I have a love for her I didn't have before."

I could not understand what had happened to me until the weekend of April 9th, 2005. My brother, Efrain, decided to go to Lubbock, Texas, with his family to buy a shofar. He is very gifted musically, and he just had to have one. They found a place called King David's. He told me that when he entered the shop, he noticed the anointing of the Lord was very strong in that place. He said a lady approached him and asked if she could help him. My brother told her he was interested in buying a shofar. She had several, and he selected one, and told her he didn't know how to play it. As she started to show him, she stopped and said, "In the Name *of Yeshua you will be playing the shofar in a week." Then, she told him, "Yahweh just said that He has directed your steps into this place." She asked my brother, "Do you know who you are?" He replied, "I think so." She asked his first name, and he said, "Efrain". Then, she asked his last name, and he said, "Rios." She took him to a computer, logged onto a website and said, "Read and learn who you are". Our last name is of direct Jewish descent. We are Sephardic (*a Jew of Spain and Portugal before the Inquisition*) Jews.*

My brother shared the above with me, and then I understood my love and the burden and passion for Israel. Because you see, Diane, it was several months before that Yahweh directed your steps into my life, and I got "messed up"! I am indebted to you for all eternity. Thank you for sharing a part of you that has enriched my life. In His service, Dee Rios

Look at God's amazing Jewish game changer – from someone who did not even know she was Jewish! To God be the Glory; great things He hath done! (And, to my sheer delight, her endorsement arrived on my birthday. God sent me a personal, priceless birthday present.)

> *Thus saith the Lord of hosts; In those days it shall come to pass, that ten men shall take hold out of all languages of the nations, even shall take hold of the skirt of him that is a Jew, saying, We will go with you: for we have heard that God is with you.* Zechariah 8:23.

Prayer: Father, we know that your Word is sure and certain! None will escape your absolutes. Genesis 12:3 is an absolute: You will bless those who bless Israel and you will curse those who curse her. You make it perfectly clear that you are ever guarding over Israel, ever watchful of man's dealings with her. Just twelve chapters from "In the beginning," you gave an ultimatum about your Chosen, and that ultimatum is just as certain today as it was the day it issued from your mouth. Father, I plead for the Church to come to a clear understanding of your will and your design for Israel. She is absolutely strategic, and it is to our advantage (promised blessings) to be watchmen on her walls. But, I do not bless her in order to receiving blessings; I bless her because you love her and, therefore, I love her. Thank you, Lord, for opening minds and hearts to this truth, and use us to perpetuate this truth throughout all the earth! In the powerful Name of Jesus, I ask this, Amen.

Picture of Naomi and Ruth from Antique Shop

15.

Praying for Israel

In 2001, Judy, a friend with a like passion for Israel, called to share that God had laid it on her heart to start a prayer group for the specific purpose of praying for Israel. What she envisioned was a starter group in our Germantown, Tennessee area, from which would spring similar groups all over the Mid-South, and ideally the world. She phoned some twenty-five committed Christians, and asked them to join her for this initial prayer meeting. Prior to that, however, she phoned me and asked if just the two of us could spend some time together seeking God's heart for this new endeavor. We decided that she would come to my house the following Tuesday morning for us to pray for God's guidance as to how He wanted the logistics handled for this group and the people He wanted involved.

I have to confess, I really did not have the same passion for this prayer venture as did Judy. There were an abundance of activities currently operating in my own little world with Christian Friends of Israel – Memphis, and taking care of our first grandchild five days a week. In addition, Ken had taken early retirement and was home most of the time. I thought that my plate was full. However, I was more than willing to help her launch this worthy new venture and to offer encouragement.

The scheduled day arrived, but certainly not as either of us could ever have imagined. She knocked on my door around 10:00 that morning, as previously planned. I opened the door and our eyes met. I saw in her the same ominous fear that gripped me. The day was already encased in a grave pallor that neither of us had ever before experienced. You see, this was that fateful nine-eleven day – September 11, 2001. The planes had already struck the tower, and the attacks were continuing. The moment-by-moment terrifying events shrouded America in the black of mourning. She and I stood speechless searching for some kind of answer each from the other.

How could it be that this was the day for the founding of this new prayer group for Israel? Was it just a coincidence?

She and I know quite well that there are no coincidences in the lives of God's children. Rather, the seriousness of the day seemed to underscore the gravity of such an undertaking. Judy and I retreated to an upstairs bedroom and closed the door so my little Rachel could crawl around safely contained. We knelt by the side of the bed and poured out heavy hearts to God for Him to establish through us a group that would faithfully gather each week and fervently pray His heart for Israel.

I remember how incredibly difficult it was to focus on praying for Israel when our own country was being so violently and needlessly attacked. But Judy and I also knew that although this was being played out on American soil by the hands of Muslim terrorists, Israel could not be far removed. We were experiencing what Israel had suffered for the whole of her existence. We now understood, first-hand, how to pray for Israel, and we also understood the seriousness with which God intended this to be taken.

This was no ordinary prayer group and could never be taken lightly; this was a Kingdom assignment. Some ten years have passed since that infamous day and the inception of our little Prayer Group for Israel, and we continue to meet faithfully every week in Germantown, Tennessee.

Even though most of the ladies in the group have gone through their own intense personal tragedies over these ten years, the focus remains ever the same: to pray for the Peace of Jerusalem; to pray for the Prime Minister; to pray for the return of precious captured soldiers; to pray for the safety of the military; to pray for eyes to see, ears to hear and hearts to understand; to pray that Israel would be the prophesied light to the Gentiles; to pray for protection for her people; to pray for the return of the Temple Mount; to pray for the third Temple to be built; to pray for the people walking in darkness to see the Great Light; and on and on. Is it easy to pray for people on the other side of the world that you do not know and probably will never know when your own life is possibly in dire circumstances? In the ten years of this group's existence, we have had a family member serve time in prison, grandchildren abused, other family members with physical and mental issues, joblessness, substance abuse, a church split, children going through divorce, and on and on.

How can individuals enduring such adversities come together to pray for the needs of others who are not family, friends or even acquaintances? I must confess that at times it is incredibly hard to focus, but something out of this world seems to happen every week when this group of like-minded people in one accord and passionate about God's business meets to pray. We tap into a power source beyond our own reach. When it is unquestionably God's assignment, and His children are in one accord, it is as though the forces of Heaven and the forces of earth collide on an unseen battlefield, and the Kingdom emerges the victor every time.

We try to view Israel from God's perspective – past, present and future – and pray accordingly. He chose her for Himself, and although there have been painful gaps in the relationship, and although at times God may have turned His back, we know from His Word that there is yet a joyful restoration promised. This is prophesied over and over in Scripture, and we pray those Scriptures back to the God of Abraham, Isaac and Jacob. We know the Temple will be rebuilt because the Bible says as much, so we pray for the Lord to sweep the Temple Mount so it can become a reality. We remind Him of the beauty of His Chosen, and pray for Him to restore the years the locusts have eaten. Oh, we pray so many, many ways! Oftentimes, He will use things that have happened to one or more of us personally in the distant past or in our current circumstances as the guide for how to pray that day.

One experience that comes to mind occurred many years ago when Ken and I were with dear friends, Don and Ann, in Colorado on a skiing trip. We had use of a house on top of a mountain not far from the slopes for a whole week. It was picture perfect. The snow was so high that it came to the tops of the bottom floor windows. It was truly breathtaking.

On this particular day (marked for me by God), the four of us had skied all morning and had stopped at a snack area for lunch. We took a leisurely break to refuel and rest, and then prepared to return to the slopes. I had all of my layers back on and lacked only my ski cap. With goggles dangling from my right wrist, and cap in both hands, I flung the cap up and over my head, and in doing so, thrust the corner of the goggles directly into the pupil of my right eye (taking tissue out of my pupil, as I would later discover). The pain was excruciating! It was like none I had ever experienced. There are no words to describe such instant and debilitating pain.

The others tried to persuade me to see a doctor, but I was convinced that if I kept my eye closed and gave it time, it would heal itself. I urged the others to go ahead without me, and I would stay there and rest. I could not open my eye without intense, gripping pain; it was unrelenting. Interestingly, too, that eye never stopped weeping – and not just a trickle – it poured. I persevered all afternoon and even through most of dinner that evening, but it was at dinner that we decided I had to see a doctor.

We drove to the emergency facility in town and soon saw the doctor on call. He put some drops in the eye to deaden the pain (praise God), and told me that I had lost possibly fifteen percent of my vision. He taped a patch over my eye that I had to wear for a week and sent me off with more drops.

Needless to say, I was out of commission for the remainder of the trip, but I gained firsthand knowledge from that experience of what it means when the Bible calls Israel the *apple of God's eye* (Zechariah 2:12) – the focal point. The eye is extremely delicate, and if violated, the pain is excruciating. This is an incredible picture of God's relationship to Israel. God forbid that any of His true Church should play a role in hurting the apple of His eye. Rather, may we be those who administer the soothing balm of comfort and healing through our sincere prayers and genuine, unconditional love.

It is true that we pray all sorts of prayers for Israel, oftentimes because we can relate in some particular way, but we are also keenly aware of the command God gave concerning her. In Genesis 12:3, God said that *He would bless those who bless Israel and curse those who curse her*. His mind has not changed. This is unalterable. But, as resolute as this Scripture is, even this is not reason enough for the weekly prayer gatherings. We do it not in order to receive blessings, but because we know God's heart for His Chosen – we do it for Him. He is our Purpose. And, He obviously loves these prayer meetings because He shows up and usually makes His presence known each week as our persistent little group of ladies pounds away at the gates of the Kingdom.

There are some ten ladies in the group, which has seen several others come and go through the years. At 10:00 in the morning, we all arrive at the serene home of one of the members. There is coffee and hot tea waiting, and as none of us has seen each other all week, there is a buzz as we try and catch up on the new move for one, the sick daughter-in-law for another, the political exploits of yet another. Then, our ever-mindful-of-the-real-purpose hostess ushers us into the living room where she pulls from our Jerusalem bag an oversized Israeli flag, which is spread over our laps. In one corner of the flag in an out-of-the-way place is monogrammed *For Such A Time As This*, the name we have given our group. In the center is placed a large, clear plastic bag containing numerous items collected over the years – a running list of all the Jewish people God brings into our paths, pictures of strategic people, Jews in harm's way, a stone from the site of an ongoing battle front in Israel. Someone will begin by praising our Great and Awesome God for His unspeakable goodness and for His tender mercies, and then the mystery begins. Before long the prayer meeting takes on its own unique character for that day as something may be spoken from which the others begin to springboard. It is as though we somehow find that strategic zone where God desires us to be, and we hover there where one after the other, realizing the vein in which we are to be praying, jumps in as the Spirit directs. It truly is a mystery. It is all about the apple of His eye and His yearning heart for His Chosen. It is never about any of us – no matter the current, personal crisis.

Oftentimes, someone will take their Bible and pray a particular Scripture they may have seen during the week that spoke to them of Israel. A small fraction of those include: Exodus 6:8; Daniel 9:4b-19; Psalm 89:34; Isaiah 54:17; Zechariah 2:8; Jeremiah 23:3; Exodus 4:22; Zechariah 12:10; Psalm 122:6-7; Isaiah 62:1; Matthew 9:37-38; Romans 11:29. It is a prayer meeting like none other, and although I have moved some forty-five minutes away, it is one of my spiritual activities for which sacrifices are made. I never intended to be a permanent fixture in that prayer group, but now I cannot imagine my life without it.

You may be thinking, "Where is the Jewish game changer in this?" It is there – just lurking. You see, there is one more interesting aspect about our group, and that is we have two famous people among our members – at least they are famous to us. We have two Jewish ladies – one Orthodox and one Messianic. (Only God could have engineered this!) We absolutely love these two ladies. Their Jewish identity lends much richness, not to mention uniqueness, to every gathering. Their presence attests to the validity and the genuineness for which we pray weekly for Israel. They would not be meeting with us and wasting their time if these were self-serving, personal agenda prayer meetings. Our little Prayer Group for Israel was founded exclusively for the purpose of praying for Israel and the Jewish people, from which we have never deviated. We delight each week to see His Word in action: *How good and pleasant it is for brothers to dwell together in unity* (Psalm 133:1). Where God and His agenda are the absolute, unity transcends all barriers.

> *I have set watchmen upon thy walls, O Jerusalem, which shall never hold their peace day nor night: ye that make mention of the Lord, keep not silence, and give him no rest, till he establish, and till he make Jerusalem a praise in the earth.* Isaiah 62:6-7.

Prayer: Father, thank you for the instrument of prayer, but, we truly do not grasp its power, do we? We just cannot fathom the out-of-this-world resource we have available to us through this medium, can we? Your Word says prayer is a vast treasure that is liberally given to each of us, yet we are so weak in its implementation. Please help us, Lord, to break through the personally constructed, needless barriers we've set up and tap into that liberal, spiritual wellspring of oneness with you.

And, thank you Lord for the multiplied power of corporate prayer which is all the more elevated when the body is unified and the masks are off and transparency is everyone's spiritual makeup. Oh, Father, for your Name's sake, let us delight to tap into your power source and call into being those things that do not yet exist. Teach us to pray, and in particular, teach us to pray for Israel. What a high calling! Lord God Almighty, awaken your precious, sleeping

Church to this calling. May she be a mighty band that will "never hold her peace day or night" for your dear Israel's sake. In the Name that is above all names I pray, Amen.

16.

Pennies

On November 14, 1993, I had an alarming dream or vision, the effects of which continue to play out in my life today. In this vision I was not only a spectator, but, in some sense, I was also a participant. What I saw was a very compelling figure that I knew intuitively as Father Jacob. He was tall with white hair, a white beard and was clothed in a long robe. I did not speak to him or to anyone. All eyes were fastened on Father Jacob; it was obvious that this was a personage that commanded full attention. I was completely entranced by him. However, something quite unimaginable began to take place. As I watched from my vantage point, absolutely riveted to him, he began to fall slowly forward. I became extremely alarmed, frantically looking around for someone to come and save him from what I knew would be an horrendous fall. But there was no one. It played out in slow motion, and that was the frustrating part because there was time for help, but none came, not even from himself. It was as though he was frozen with no ability to so much as extend his arms and brace his fall. His face-forward fall was so powerful that the earth shook beneath my feet. It was a horrible sight. And, going through my mind as I watched it all was the fact that no one could survive such a fall. Afterward, I went over to him, not hurriedly, but cautiously, all the while praying fervently for God's help, pleading, "Please, Lord, let him be alive." I knelt over him to look into his face, and shockingly there in the place of his face was a wheat penny (American pennies minted between 1909 and 1958), and then I came to myself.

I was visibly shaken and troubled by what I had witnessed. Everything about this scene was terrifying – and what I found most confusing was that wheat penny! I wrote it all down, as I have come to understand I must do, and pondered it at length, not telling anyone for the longest time what I had seen.

Over the next few weeks, I set out to study the wheat penny and discovered some very interesting facts. This penny was designed by a Jewish man, Victor David Brenner, who was born in Lithuania in 1871. The coin was first circulated in 1909 and immediately came under attack because Mr. Brenner prominently displayed his initials on the coin, as had other coin designers. His initials were soon removed. His greatest opponent was the chief engraver of the U. S. Mint, Charles E. Barber. After Mr. Barber's death in 1918, Mr. Brenner's initials once again appeared on the wheat penny, though not as conspicuously as on the original. A lesser reported version said the outcry arose over his initials because he was Jewish. I thought that cruelly interesting, if it were so.

Following is the text of Mr. Brenner's letter to Mr. Farran Zerbe, President of the American Numismatic Association from 1908 – 1910:

New York
August 23, 1909

My Dear Mr. Zerbe:
It is mighty hard for me to express my sentiments with reference to the initials on the cent. The name of the artist on a coin is essential for the student of history as it enables him to trace environments and conditions of the time said coin was produced. Much fume has been made about my initials as a means of advertisement; such is not the case. The very talk the initials has brought out has done more good for numismatics than it could do me personally.

The cent not alone represents in part my art, but it represents the type of art of our period.

The conventionalizing of the sheafs of wheat was done by me with much thought, and I feel that with the prescribed wording no better design could be obtained. The cent will wear out two of the last lines in time, due entirely to the hollow surface.

The original design had Brenner on it, and that was changed to the initials. Of course the issue rests with the numismatic bodies . . .

Very sincerely Yours,
(signed)
Victor D. Brenner

As I thought of the penny and what connections there might be between it and the Father Jacob or Israel (God later changed Jacob's name to Israel) in my vision, I pondered that the penny is the smallest denomination of our currency, just as Israel is one of the world's smallest nations – only about the size of New Jersey. I also mused that to most, a penny is insignificant. It is nothing to see someone step right over one because it is not worth the effort to stoop and pick up. The truth of the matter is that in today's economy, it costs more to make a penny than it is worth. It is viewed by some as a financial drain, and how intriguing that at its very inception, enmity arose!

Contrast that with how many view Israel. They think nothing of stepping over her. In their minds she costs more than she is worth. They see her as a financial drain. And there certainly was enmity at her inception. The correlations are quite intriguing.

Just know that because of my calling to love and pray for Israel, the penny is now extremely significant to me. As a matter of fact, every time I find one, I view it as my prompt to pray for Israel. And after that experience I began finding pennies – and looking for them – everywhere. I remember one incident in particular when Ken and I were on vacation and were going to a public laundry to wash clothes. As I stepped from our car with my armload of clothes, I discovered beneath my feet a pile of pennies, as though someone had dumped them out as you would an ashtray.

My most interesting penny incident occurred one Wednesday while in our little prayer group for Israel. I had worn loafers that day, and you will recall from the previous game changer that there are two Jewish ladies in our group. As we were in our circle intently praying for Israel, Judi (a Messianic, believing Jew) took her purse and began scrounging around in it. She then dropped to her knees in front of me and proceeded to put pennies in my penny loafers. I looked at her and said, "Judi, you have no idea what you are doing." I told the group about my vision or dream, and they seemed somewhat amazed at the whole scenario, but I was overwhelmed. I was almost fearful because I knew there was much more going on behind the scenes than was immediately visible. I deposited this little incident in my spiritual penny bank, wondering where God was going with it.

A couple of years later, I received an interesting e-mail from a middle school teacher at Horn Lake Middle School (Horn Lake, Mississippi), introducing herself and writing that she had been given my name as someone who might be able to help her school enlist a Holocaust survivor to come and speak to their students who were doing Holocaust studies. I happily put her in touch with the Memphis Jewish Federation, who eagerly accommodated by providing not just one, but two, speakers for their students.

This teacher, Susan Powell, and I continued emailing back and forth. In our exchange of correspondence, she poured out her heart about her students. She said that these students are precious to her, and informed me that this is one of the lowest income schools in the area. She said that many of these students felt they would never amount to anything (because that was what they had been told), which broke her heart. She said that she would love for them to do a project for the Holocaust. I told her I had some ideas, so we agreed to meet the following Sunday afternoon at a local coffee shop. She said there was another teacher at Horn Lake Middle School, Melissa Swartz, who also taught Holocaust studies, and asked if she could join us, which, of course, was perfectly alright with me.

We met and introduced ourselves, and then the teachers began to share about their sincere concerns for their students and their desire for these students to have a real Holocaust project. When they finished, they looked at me as if to say, "Now, who are you and what is your story?" I told them some of the things in which our little group had been involved, and particularly about *The Remembering*, our children's Holocaust exhibit. I showed them a few pictures of that project, and then showed them something I had made just for myself.

When we closed the doors on *The Remembering* that final time, my heart felt as though it would break in two. I hated with everything in me to end such a successful, unifying exhibit. But, our allotted time was up. It had been extremely demanding, not just the four weeks it ran, but that coupled with the many months of preparation beforehand. Ken had an extended trip out West planned for us, and he could not wait for some R&R. It was tearing me apart, though, to have to transition from that highly charged, all-consuming event to a personal pleasure trip. Who would not welcome the magnificence and the grandeur of the Grand Canyon over daily hearing those voices in the first room telling of their surviving the Holocaust as a child? Of course I wanted to experience those great American wonders, but I needed some time to process all that had transpired during that month. However, that was not meant to be. So, to appease and comfort myself, and to hold on to that exhibit a bit longer, and also as a means of somehow grasping the enormity of the one and a half million children who died in the Holocaust, I decided to do a little personal, visual aid. I took a clear plastic tray with sides, 11x14 inches, and placed a pattern of the Israeli flag in the bottom. Then, as we travelled, we would stop along the way for me to buy plain blue and white birthday candles, which I used to completely fill in the tray (creating a blue and white Israeli flag). What I discovered from my little experiment was that this size box held 3,528 candles, and that to produce the needed 1.500,000 would take 425 of these same-sized containers, which would cover a 21x21 square-foot room. (And remember that each small, regular-sized birthday candle represents a child, a real person denied their God-given right to life.) This project helped me to put that overwhelming figure into perspective and also kept me linked with the project a little longer.

When I met with Susan and Melissa, I took along my little birthday candle experiment. When I pulled it from the bag to show, I could tell their wheels were rapidly beginning to turn. I told them that wax candles are not ideal; they melt and are much more expensive than I had ever imagined. However, I told them there was something they could collect a million and a half of, and which basically would be free – people would give them away willingly. They were all ears, and then I said they could collect pennies. The two teachers became like giddy schoolgirls, bubbling over with excitement.

Then, Melissa turned to me and said, "Did you know my husband is Jewish?" Of course, I did not; I had never met either of these ladies before. Then, Melissa said, "And, did you know he is an artist and can work in any medium – even pennies?" What a Jewish game changer God dropped into my little unsuspecting world that day! This was more than huge; it was absolutely God-sized! To some extent I grasped the enormity of the moment, but wondered if either of these teachers had even a hint. The project was born in that moment and has since taken on the name *The Unknown Child* (www.unknownchild.com).

As of this writing, about 18 months after that initial meeting, we have some 1,300,000 pennies, all but about 200,000 ($2,000). The children bring in their snack money and have contests between classes. They have written letters to politicians, sports figures and movie stars. Containers have been placed in several businesses around the area, including the Jewish Community Center and the Memphis Jewish Home in Memphis. There have been articles in local newspapers and a local Jewish magazine, church participation, and the students have had two appearances on one of the early morning TV programs. A nearby home school group has jumped onboard and raised over $1,000 with a car wash, door-to-door solicitation and giving the proceeds from their year-end carnival. Recently the project was supercharged when the Jewish owner of a downtown mall donated all the coins from the mall fountain. The students were shown on that early morning TV program, WREG "Live @ 9," fishing for coins in the fountain.

Michael Swartz, our "connected" Jewish artist, has presented us with a preliminary sketch of the proposed project. It shows a woman tightly holding a child seated next to her. The verse we see depicting this sketch is found in Jeremiah 31:15, *A voice was heard in Ramah, lamentation, and bitter weeping; Rachel weeping for her children refused to be comforted for her children, because they were not.* (Rachel here represents Israel.)

Of course, there are many hurdles yet to cross and many puzzle pieces still to fall into place, but there is no doubt that God is the Originator and Orchestrator of this endeavor, and its completion will assuredly be realized, no doubt pulling into its wake furthered unity between Jew and Gentile and needed education of the horrendous atrocities of the Holocaust.

On this marvelous journey of collecting 1,500,000 pennies (which sum, by the way, will weigh between four and six tons), there have been many incredible stories. For example, Ken and I were thrilled when the church we attend agreed to collect pennies for a month.

Normally, when I gather pennies from various collection sites, I do not count them. We want the students to have the hands-on experience in order for them to better understand the massive number of lost lives. However, because I wanted to report back to our church the total, I elected to count those. One Sunday afternoon, my Daddy and one of our sons and I gathered around the kitchen table with the pile of pennies before us, ready to count. I was not prepared for our eerie discovery. We pulled from the pile two German coins – both from the Holocaust era. One was a 1931 penny (interestingly with a sheaf of wheat on it), and the other a 1940 nickel bearing a swastika. Only God!

Is anything too hard for the Lord? Genesis 18:14a.

Prayer: Father, there is no doubt that this is your assignment. No one else orchestrates like you do. We love watching your masterpiece unfold and play out before our very eyes. We also love being involved in our Father's business. How good you are to us; how tender are your mercies toward us. Thank you for including in your Kingdom work all the "whosoevers" out there who want to come. Thank you that you are no respecter of persons, and that what you desire is sincerity in the innermost parts. Lord, may we give you our best, our all! You alone are worthy, and we ascribe to you all majesty, praise and adoration. Thank you for loving us. Oh, God, that we could love you in return with the love you so richly deserve! To the only, all-wise God be glory, power and dominion forever and ever! In the blessed Name of Jesus, I pray, Amen.

Sketch of the Unknown Child by Michael Swartz

Jeremiah 31:15: *A voice was heard in Ramah, lamentation, and bitter weeping; Rachel weeping for her children refused to be comforted for her children, because they were not.*

17.

Is it For Jews Only?

This Jewish game changer, above all the others, is the one I have most desired to share with you. It is also the one I have most dreaded because I was unsure that, in writing, I would be able to adequately express its immeasurable importance. Even now I am fervently pleading with the Lord to write this one through me: *"Father, please, for all Christian families everywhere, help us to understand this most basic, yet most profound and life-changing of all Jewish traditions."*

Last year Ken and I were privileged to be invited to the home of one of Memphis' most prominent Jewish families for Shabbat. We were working with this family's son on an area-wide Israel festival, and this was the weekend of the event. There were several out-of-town dignitaries attending and various other scheduled activities coinciding with the festival. Some 30 people were expected for Shabbat, and Ken and I were privileged to be seated next to the hosts (even now as I write, I am shaking my head in disbelief).

From our seats, we had the perfect vantage point from which to observe everything. What they did on this particular Friday evening is what they do on all Friday evenings, although probably not to so great an extent. This Sabbath may have seemed more special because of the large number of guests present and the extra food prepared, but it was not. What made this Sabbath special is what makes all Sabbaths special: It is the day set apart by God Himself. It is His appointed, holy, sacred day.

At sundown, our hostess lit the two Shabbat candles, welcoming in the appointed day, and then the family went to synagogue. After services, they returned home to receive the guests as they arrived and to fellowship and enjoy the festive meal. We were all seated at a fully extended, seemingly never-ending table. Our host took the bread (challah), broke it and passed it around. He then took the wine and blessed and drank it, and we all followed in like manner. He read blessings for the occasion from small booklets on the table, available to all. Our host and hostess eagerly shared with us the details of what they were doing and why. Truly, it was an honor!

Ken and I had been guests at many Shabbat dinners (mostly in homes of Messianic Jews), so this was neither foreign nor uncomfortable for us. Yet, each family has its own, unique way of observing the Sabbath, so there are always nuggets to be gleaned.

After the blessings and readings, we feasted on a sumptuous meal. The hostess shared with us that each week, starting as early as Wednesday, she begins preparation of the family's favorite dishes. Even though she has household help, she makes all of the food herself, and it was obvious that this was a role in which she took great pleasure.

As the evening progressed, I observed something very intriguing. (At special times like this, I try diligently to take in everything, never wanting to miss a thing.) Toward the end of the meal, the father (our host for the evening) rose from the table and went over to his grown son and whispered something into his ear. Then, a short while later, I watched as this son went over and whispered something into his own grown son's ear, and after that, into his daughter's ear. I knew what was transpiring because I knew this tradition; however, this was my first time to personally witness it. These fathers were whispering the Aaronic blessing into their children's ears – grown or not. This blessing is found in Numbers 6:22-27: *And the Lord spake unto Moses, saying, Speak unto Aaron and unto his sons, saying, On this wise ye shall bless the children of Israel, saying unto them, "The Lord bless thee, and keep thee: The Lord make his face shine upon thee, and be gracious unto thee: The Lord lift up his countenance upon thee, and give thee peace".* <u>And they shall put my name upon the children of Israel; and I will bless them</u>.

(I love the ongoing lessons the Lord gives me through Naomi. When I finished my first draft of this manuscript, I mailed her a copy to sign-off on. I would never want to offend her in any regard, and I had to know that she was okay with the different things that I had written about her. There was one change that she asked to be made, and it was made. Several days later the phone rang, and it was she again. Naomi told me that her husband was reading the manuscript and had an issue with something. My mind began frantically searching for the offense. I surmised that he might think I had overstepped my bounds in my relationship with his dear wife. I instantly began pleading with the Lord to have mercy. I just knew in that moment that this whole book would have to be shelved.

Naomi said (addressing her husband's concerns), "I don't understand you Christians." "We would never say, 'Moses said. . .' You give far too much credit to man. Instead, we would say, 'The Lord said through Moses (or Aaron) . . .'" She is absolutely correct. My saying the "Aaronic blessing" was offensive because they felt I was giving the credit to Aaron and not to God.)

God's blessing through Moses/Aaron is reportedly the greatest blessing in the Bible because it is the only one composed by God and dictated to Moses to be placed on the children of Israel forever. God told Moses that when you put this blessing on the people, <u>you put His Name on them and He will bless them</u>.

Recently, I heard Dr. John Garr (author of *Blessings for Family and Friends*) speak on this subject on Jewish Voice TV with host Rabbi Jonathan Bernis. Dr. Garr said, "There was a study done to try and understand why the Jewish people seem to excel on a percapita basis far more than any other people group. The final conclusion of the study revealed that the only thing done differently in Jewish homes is that their children are directly blessed by their parents". Dr. Garr also shared that this blessing was designed to be spoken in the context of the family.

That was what I was privileged to witness on this Shabbat – the father blessing his son, who in turn blessed his own son and daughter (all of whom were adults). They were obeying God's millennia-old command. And, this prominent family, by all visible signs, is indeed blessed far beyond my knowing or ability to convey.

Two of our dearest friends, Jon and Mary Jane, were also present that evening and just as keenly taking in all of the events. The four of us came away with the desperate, sinking feeling that our own families had been robbed because we had not been taught this foundational principle, and had not passed it on to our own children.

They have had family issues, too, but certainly not to the extent as have Ken and I. The four of us left wondering, "What if ..."

Jon has connections with a prominent religious organization that is a Christian-based rehab facility for drug and alcohol abuse. Because of his affiliation, and because of the impact of that Shabbat evening, he had an overwhelming desire to bring all the residents at this facility into his home, and ask this Jewish man (our host for that evening), if he would come and put the coveted blessing on them – as he had done all the many years for his own children. The man graciously consented; the event was scheduled, and, thankfully, Ken and I had another invitation.

The special occasion arrived, as did all the invitees. Jon and Mary Jane grilled out hamburgers and hot dogs (kosher, of course), and the young men seemed to thoroughly enjoy their evening out. Jon called everyone to attention and introduced the special guest – our Jewish host – and explained the purpose for the gathering and the blessing each would receive, passing out copies of the blessing for them to keep. Then, our Jewish host went to each young man (about twenty present), and whispered the blessing into their ear. These men were the down and outs, and this rehab facility may very well have been their last stop before prison or worse. I wondered if they had any idea of the incredible privilege afforded them, and I also wondered what profound effects this evening might have on their lives.

I retreated to the kitchen to attend to my KP duties, and shortly one of the young men came in and began talking to me. Usually I am somewhat reserved around unfamiliar people, and as he chatted, I marveled that he could be so outgoing and so open with a complete stranger – an older woman at that. He proceeded to tell me that he was a chef and insisted on writing out one of his favorite recipes for me – Asparagus Parmesan. When I took the recipe from him and read his name, I was astonished. My mouth dropped open. He had written, "Abraham Israel Cohen" (altered slightly to protect his identity). "Are you Jewish?" I asked. He said he was. Still in shock, I said, "So, you understand what is going on here tonight?" I asked. And, of course, he said he did. I asked him if he grew up with his father blessing him. His countenance immediately fell, and in obvious personal anguish he said that his father had stopped blessing him when he was in his early teens. I wondered if quite possibly he felt as though he was where he was in life because an invaluable tradition, or, rather, command, had been halted when he most needed it. I saw the pain in this young man's face, and my heart broke right along with his. This was, for me, a very grievous Jewish game changer.

Many months later, unable to let go of all the events that occurred those two indelible evenings, I decided it was time to institute the same tradition in our home. We had inordinately more than our share of family issues, and I determined that every Friday evening I would put this same, commanded blessing on each member of our family, present or away.

Did I understand what I was doing? Absolutely not! But, recently our dear pastor said that you do not understand and then obey, but you obey in order to understand. Would I ever understand the journey on which I was embarking? Possibly not, but our family was in desperate need of blessings, and what better blessing than the one – the only one – dictated and commanded by God to be put on His people?

That first Friday evening, I brought out two Shabbat candles (found in the Kosher section of larger supermarkets), and lit them and blessed the day and then specifically put the Aaronic blessing dictated by God on each member of our family, naming them one by one. I did it before anyone arrived home, because I did not want them to see me and think I had completely lost it – again. The following Friday night, I did the same thing, except this time, I had to take the candles back to our bedroom and hide in the closet to light them, because some of the family had already come in. I did not want them to think this Christian had gone all Jewish crazy on them.

Throughout the following week I was haunted by what I had done. Scripture gnawed at me: the one that tells you to put your candle on a lamp stand for all to see and not to hide it under a basket (Matthew 5:15). Hiding the candles was exactly what I had done. So, that next Friday came, and I prayed earnestly for the Lord to give me boldness to light the candles and pray the blessing in front of the family, and I asked that there would be no raised eyebrows or stealing glances. When Ken and I and two of our sons, who were with us that evening, sat down for dinner, I brought out the candles and the matches and said that I was going to put God's blessing through Aaron on each member of the family, and explained why. Ken chimed in and said, "This is our home and this is what we do in our home." I nearly fell out! Oh, how good God was to allow Ken to endorse this! God specifically answered my prayer! I knew from Ken's backing me that God wanted this in our Christian home, just as He did in all the many Jewish homes around the world.

We have continued the candle lighting and the commanded blessing each Friday evening since. Is it a ritual? Far from it! On the contrary, it is a deliberate gesture of obediently and determinedly placing God's Name on each member of our precious family – present or away. I recently heard it said that many things that seem so simple have the most profound consequences. Have we robbed our homes and our families by not observing this simple command?

One final comment: In Hebrews 11, the chapter of the giants of faith, two entrants are listed of whom it was said that they blessed their children (verses 20 and 21). If this act was important enough to land them in the Hall of Faith chapter, should it not also warrant our serious consideration? It is not just the mere blessing of our children, but blessing them with the only God-commanded, God-dictated words specifically designed for the purpose of placing His Name on His people? Paul says in Romans 1:16: . . . *to the Jew first, and also to the Greek*.

> *The Lord bless thee, and keep thee: The Lord make his face shine upon thee, and be gracious unto thee: The Lord lift up his countenance upon thee, and give thee peace.*
> Numbers 6:24-26.

Prayer: Oh, God Almighty, have mercy on us, your children, and grant us wisdom and knowledge and understanding in all that we do, especially in our dealings with family. May we not miss anything you have for us as we go through this life – especially treasures meant for our family's good. Father, we bless you and humbly thank you for all your unspeakable gifts, especially for showcasing this particular blessing. To you be all honor and power and glory and praise forever, world without end! In the sweet and only Name of Jesus I pray, Amen.

Israel Cohen

Asparagas
Fresh Asparagas
Black Pepper Corn
Garlic Salt
Balsamic Vinegerette
Olive Oil

Cooking Instructions

Wrap in Tin Foil. Place in Oven at 325° for 15 to 20 until tender. Open and pour out the juice. Put on Platter and Cover with graded Parm and enjoy

Mr. Cohen's Asparagus Parmesan Recipe

18.

Provoking to Jealousy

One cannot frequent the world of Judaism very long before discovering the number "eighteen." In my Hebrew classes, I learned the importance placed on numbers, and also learned that all Hebrew words can be converted to numbers because all letters have assigned numeric value. The first letter of the Hebrew alphabet is *aleph*, and its numeric value is one. The second is *bet*, and its numeric value is two, and so on (with variations). The point I am making is that all Hebrew words have a number equivalency.

A very important word in Judaism is "life," and its numeric value is eighteen. Because of such, monetary gifts are often given in increments of eighteen. An appropriate bar or bat mitzvah gift bearing a sensitivity to Judaism is $18 or $180, or anything divisible by eighteen ($36, $54, and so on). This is also true for wedding gifts, baby gifts, etc. Interestingly, the cost of planting a tree in Israel (as a memorial or a tribute) is $18. My 91-year old father died recently, and a dear friend had a grove of trees (ten) planted in his memory – $180. There is a high regard for the number eighteen in Judaism, just as there is a high regard for life.

Because of the importance of the number eighteen, I had hoped that when all was said and done, and all game changers recollected, there would be eighteen. I wanted no finagling, no coercion, no making it happen; I simply wanted eighteen, no more and no less. For me, I think it was somewhat of having God's stamp of approval on this book. Praise Ha Shem (do you recall that from chapter nine – The Name?), there were the eighteen chapters I had hoped for. I will never get over His tenderness and His sensitivity to detail. Thank you Father.

There is a little known, rarely taught command that was given to the Church some two thousand years ago known as provoking to jealousy (the term used in the King James Version). I dare say that if you queried one hundred active, evangelical Christians as to what "provoking to jealousy" is and the last time they were conscious of God using them in that role, their only response would probably be a confused, glazed stare. What is provoking to jealousy, and is it really a command given to the Church? Paul is the New Testament authority on this subject, and is the one from whom we will seek answers.

Following are excerpts from Romans 10:18 – 11:33, taken from The Living Bible:

> *But what about the Jews? Have they heard God's Word? Yes, for it has gone wherever they are; the Good News has been told to the ends of the earth. And did they understand [that God would give his salvation to others if they refused to take it]? Yes, for even back in the time of Moses, God had said that he would make his people <u>jealous</u> and try to wake them up by giving his salvation to the foolish heathen nations. And later on Isaiah said boldly that God would be found by people who weren't even looking for him. In the meantime, he keeps on reaching out his hands to the Jews, but they keep arguing and refusing to come. . . . So this is the situation: Most of the Jews have not found the favor of God they are looking for. A few have . . . but the eyes of the others have been blinded. This is what our Scriptures refer to when they say that God has put them to sleep, shutting their eyes and ears so that they do not understand what we are talking about when we tell them of Christ. And so it is to this very day. . . . Does this mean that God has rejected his Jewish people forever? Of course not! His purpose was to make his salvation available to the Gentiles, and then the Jews would be <u>jealous</u> and begin to want God's salvation for themselves. . . . As you know, God has appointed me (Paul) as a special messenger to you Gentiles. . . . so that if possible I can <u>make them want what you Gentiles have</u> and in that way save some of them. . . . When God turned away from them it meant that he turned to the rest of the world to offer his salvation; and now it is even more wonderful when the*

Jews come to Christ. It will be like dead people coming back to life. . . . Now many of the Jews are enemies of the Gospel. They hate it. But this has been a benefit to you, for it has resulted in God's giving his gifts to you Gentiles. Yet the Jews are still beloved of God because of his promises to Abraham, Isaac, and Jacob. For God's gifts and his call can never be withdrawn; he will never go back on his promises. Once you were rebels against God, but when the Jews refused his gifts, God was merciful to you instead. And now the Jews are the rebels, but some day they, too, will share in God's mercy upon you. For God has given them all up to sin so that he could have mercy upon all alike. Oh, what a wonderful God we have! How great are his wisdom and knowledge and riches! How impossible it is for us to understand his decisions and his methods!

From the Apostle Paul's writings, it is undeniably clear that all believers are fully equipped to provoke to jealousy. We make those on the outside jealous for what we have simply by living unhindered, Christ-infused lives boldly and openly before Jews and before all people. Is provoking to jealousy broadly taught in churches today? When was the last time the above-average Christian (those passionately pursuing the things of the Lord) asked for this assignment? Most of us, if presented with the opportunity, would be at a complete loss as to what to do or how to do it. If encountered with this opportunity, we would probably not even recognize it, and I would have been at the top of the list before the Lord thrust me on this unimaginable journey.

The term "provoking to jealousy" (as used in the King James Version), is foreign to most Christians, and Paul must have understood the impending problem because of his warning, "*I do not want you to be ignorant of this mystery*" (Romans 11:25a - KJV). Sad to say that the mystery (Jews denouncing what was rightfully theirs, thereby allowing Gentiles to be grafted in, which in turn provokes Jews to jealousy) escapes virtually all Christians today. We are ignorant of God's desired outcome: that He could have mercy upon all alike (Romans 11:32). Because provoking to jealousy remains a mystery, it goes without saying that the vast majority of Christians are not on assignment. When was the last time any of us woke up in the mornings and prayed, "Lord, your Word says I am to be provoking to jealousy, so would you please send me a precious Jewish person, or anyone else, who I can lovingly provoke to jealousy?"

This seems more like no man's land, does it not? But, wait until you see how easily it is accomplished. God illustrated provoking to jealousy to me on two different occasions. The first instance occurred when I was privileged to witness a dialogue between a world-renowned Orthodox Rabbi and an equally high-profile, lay evangelical Christian. The Christian hammered away at the Rabbi, telling him that it was a Christian's responsibility to try and convert him. The Rabbi listened patiently, waiting his turn, and when the Christian finally ran out of steam, the Rabbi responded, "I've read the New Testament. I know what Paul says about Gentiles provoking Jews to jealousy, but you have been trying it your way for two thousand years, and it hasn't worked. Now, let me tell you how to provoke me to jealousy: **if you will just love me, you will provoke me to jealousy**." His words exploded inside me! What an amazing Jewish game changer! What a phenomenal lesson for the Church! But why should the Rabbi's simplistic yet powerful response be surprising? Isn't that exactly what Jesus taught? *"And thou shalt love the Lord thy God with all thy heart, with all thy soul, and with all thy mind, and with all thy strength . . . and thy neighbor as thyself . . . there is no other commandment greater,"* (Mark 12:30-31). This love about which Jesus was teaching and the Rabbi was speaking is *unconditional* love, the only love that is truly Biblical, and commanded. Sadly, though, the Rabbi's invitation to love him seemed to completely evade the Christian. Oh, how grievous are our missed opportunities!

Can we love – unconditionally? If so, then we are ready for our provoking to jealousy assignment; we have all the necessary tools. And, thankfully, we do not have to be Bible scholars, which God understands most of us are not. If that were a criterion, about ninety-nine per cent of us would be left at the starting gate.

The other occasion when I witnessed a Christian provoking to jealousy was when I had received word that the husband of a dear, Orthodox Jewish friend of mine had died. Most Jewish funerals occur within twenty-four hours of death because they do not embalm. They take literally the Genesis 3:19 passage, "... *for dust thou art, and unto dust shalt thou return.*" I was thankful for the call because most times it is too late to attend services if you find out about the death in the newspaper.

This funeral was held in a small chapel on the grounds of a Jewish cemetery. After the service, we walked directly to the adjacent burial site. When everyone was in place, the Rabbi said a few words, the Cantor chanted, and the burial commenced. The Jewish leaders in charge placed the coffin in the ground and covered it with the mandatory concrete slab, followed by the dirt. There were hired laborers to come in afterward and complete the task, but the work was done primarily by the Jewish men officiating.

We had had torrential rains in Memphis the day before, and the grounds were completely saturated. They were not shoveling dirt; it was literally mud. I was on the sidelines taking in everything. The Rabbi shoveled a while, and then the Cantor took the shovel and made a few digs, and then another Jewish man who was part of the leadership took his turn, and so on. Then, quite by surprise, an African-American man standing in the background parted the onlookers and stepped forward. He was meticulously dressed in a light, chocolate brown suit, with a pristine white shirt and a perfectly coordinating tie. He could have been featured in a men's fashion magazine; yet, he seemed oblivious of his fine attire or the mud. He reached for the shovel, never making eye contact with the Rabbi. I was aghast. "Can he do such a thing – is that allowed?" And, he quite possibly may have entertained the same thoughts, but he did not let anything stop him. He took the shovel from the Jewish hands and began diligently filling the grave, side-by-side with the Jewish officials. The Rabbi took the final strokes, and then asked the family to line the sidewalk so that all present could file past, expressing condolences as we left the cemetery. I followed along and headed for my car, overwhelmed by what I had just witnessed.

As I proceeded to my car, it just so happened that I was walking by the uninvited grave digger. I could not restrain myself and said, "What you did truly blessed me." He seemed somewhat embarrassed, and for whatever reason said, "I'm not Jewish" (maybe to justify his actions for fear he might have overstepped his bounds). I told him I was not Jewish either, that I was a Baptist. He said, "I am a Methodist." It was obvious this conversation was making him uncomfortable. He then said in somewhat of a reprimanding tone, and probably to end the mostly one-sided conversation, "I did it because I **love** them!" He got it; he understood and exercised perfectly the provoking to jealousy command, although apparently oblivious to his role. He had cultivated a relationship with the deceased during his lifetime and then **loved** him to the end – literally.

A couple of days later, I visited in the home of this family who was sitting sheva (the seven days of mourning where the family receives those wishing to pay their respects). We were all in a large circle in the living room making light conversation when one of the Jewish ladies who had been at the funeral spoke up and said, "Something happened at the cemetery that I will never forget." Tears welled up in her eyes and began running down her cheeks. She continued, "I could not believe that man (our African-American, Methodist man) would help shovel the dirt." Many similar comments followed from all around the room, each echoing the same sentiment. That man had literally provoked to jealousy every Jew (and this Gentile) at that funeral – by his selfless, unconditional, **loving** act of servitude. He had dared to cross that invisible, yet ever-present, Jewish-Gentile dividing line and follow his heart. He dared to step out in faith. He brought Paul's charge to life – he fulfilled the command. And, incredibly, his selfless act had the ripple effect of not only touching those in attendance, but, by word of mouth, many others who had not been present that day.

How many of us are willing to step out of our comfortable Christian confines (our ruts) and cross over into that *taboo* (or so we have been taught) world of Judaism, picking up whatever lowly instrument God provides, and stoop to shovel whatever it is with which we are presented? That is the kind of person God will use on this assignment. But, surely, since Jesus stepped from His comfortable confines of Heaven and stooped to pick up the humiliating instrument of the cross for us, we can avail ourselves to Him in this possibly uncomfortable arena.

My all-time favorite verse is, *"The harvest truly is plenteous, but the labourers are few; pray ye therefore the Lord of the harvest, that he will send forth labourers into his harvest"* (Matthew 9:37).

Do we have ears that can hear the plea in this verse? Can we pray for more laborers to come into God's harvest field – even if it means us? And, incidentally, this is a red letter verse – Jesus is the Spokesman! Jesus, himself, is the One pleading for us to pray for more workers in His Father's fields. Can we, with arms reaching upward toward Heaven, exuberantly respond, "Here am I, Lord, send me!" There is no doubt that this is one exciting field, to which I can personally attest, and there is also no doubt that this field is near to the heart of God.

The prophet Jeremiah said (8:20), *"The harvest is past, the summer is ended, and we are not saved."* Oh, my friend, open your ears to God's cry and His call. Counter Jeremiah's woeful lament with, "Not in my field and not on my watch!"

Prayer: Oh Father, please forgive our insensitivity and our lack of concern in this area of Jewish-Christian relations. We do not want to be ignorant, as the Apostle Paul warned. Enlighten our minds to all truth, and take away the spirit of fear when the circumstances may be foreign. Give us the same boldness as the man at the funeral, and may we, without our ever having any consciousness of it, provoke to jealousy all who come in contact with us and who do not have a genuine, personal relationship with you. Thank you, Father, for the invitation to be in your field, and may everything we do and say in your service reflect our allegiance solely to you. All praise to the Most High God forever and ever! In the sweet Name of Jesus, Amen.

Conclusion

Many years ago, I had a most unusual dream (or vision) that, on occasion, is resurrected and replayed for my continued consideration. This was a powerful experience that I knew was from the Lord. In this dream I witnessed the progression of my spiritual journey. The setting was a row of houses on a city street. I began at the first one, and moved from house to house en route to my final destination. The houses were lined up, one after the other, and after a brief stop at one, I would move on to the next. These houses represented the different churches where Ken and I had been members. In some, there were people inside to greet me – the ones who had a personal impact on my spiritual walk. There were probably five or six such houses on my route.

At the end of these houses, yet in line with and somehow connected to them, was a man sitting outside in an old wooden ladder-back chair all by himself with a board game on his lap. He called out to me to come and play (I do love board games.), but I declined because I knew I dared not get side-tracked.

Suddenly, there was a driving force inside me, and I realized that my predictable, spiritual course, as I knew it, was about to undergo a profound transition. The status quo no longer held any allure. I knew I could not stay this course any longer, even though I loved these places and loved these people.

The total distance I covered seemed no more than one side of a city block. Each structure was on the same side of the street, one right after the other, and following the man playing the board game was an open field where there was space for more of the same-type structures to be built. Following the open field was an intersection. I reached the intersection and paused; I was at a critical juncture in my spiritual journey. I could either cross the street and continue on as usual, or I could turn to the left or to the right. I do not recall ever looking to the left, but I intuitively knew I did not want to cross the street. As I stood there trying to find my way, I was suddenly intrigued by activity some distance off to my right. As I gazed down that road, I saw a single, burning light hanging from a power line, and dark-skinned people slowly, one-by-one, beginning to gather underneath that light. It was the light and those people that held the allure for me, and so strong was the compelling that I could not be stopped. I had to go where they were. My choice was made. I turned to the right.

At this point I was conscious of Ken, my precious life partner, who was a short distance back. I had already turned right at the intersection, and he was now approaching the intersection and also had his own choice to make. I was so hopeful that he would make the same choice as I had made. After he stood there for a while, he called out to me to come back and cross the street with him, but I just could not be deterred from that light or those foreign-to-me and different-from-me people. However, I was ever-conscious of him and hopeful for the choice he would make. Then I saw him turn to the right toward me, and the dream ended.

I knew this Light and I knew these people because I had read about them in the prophet Isaiah (9:2): *The people that walked in darkness have seen a great light: they that dwell in the land of the shadow of death, upon them hath the light shined.*

Had my life up to that point been a mistake? Of course not! It was that wonderful spiritual journey that had brought me to my Savior and the Holy Scriptures. Was I merely playing games up to that point? Certainly not! My fellow church members had a positive, godly impact on my life. Oh, how tender are my thoughts toward each of those matriarchs and patriarchs. They helped mold my life. However, God had a new direction for me, and if I were to remain in that status quo position, then I would be the one playing a game, one at which I would never win.

In this dream I was the one who had to make the break; I had to determine to change my course. It is true that God's hand was heavy upon me, but the choice was still mine.

The Lord taught me so much while writing and researching my previous book (*Ruth 3,000 Years of Sleeping Prophecy Awakened*). One of the most critical and pivotal junctures in that story was also at an "intersection of choosing." It had to do with the relationship between *Jewish* Naomi and *Gentile* Ruth.

In that book, it was Gentile Ruth who stepped from her comfort zone (Moab) to embrace a foreign-to-her people (Jewish) and a different-from-her culture (Judaism). What if she, like her sister-in-law, Orpah, had never budged from Moab? Most of us are very familiar with, and many can even quote, those endearing words from Ruth to Naomi at that juncture (1:16). However, rarely, if ever, do we include the seventeenth verse – the *continuation* of Ruth's discourse. Many have even had that sixteenth verse read during their wedding ceremonies, but they omit the more ominous seventeenth verse. Let us look at all of Ruth's words: (16) *And Ruth said, Intreat me not to leave thee, or to return from following after thee: for whither thou goest, I will go; and where thou lodgest, I will lodge: thy people shall be my people, and thy God my God:* (17) *Where thou diest, will I die, and there will I be buried: the Lord do so to me, and more also, if ought but death part thee and me.* In verse sixteen and continuing into the first part of verse seventeen we see Ruth's vow to Naomi, but the latter part of verse seventeen is Ruth's vow to God. In that second vow she stated that if – for any reason, except death – she failed to keep her vow to Naomi (that of constant companionship), then God was to step in and deal with her very severely.

Who moved in the story of Ruth? Who crossed over from her comfort zone into that no-man's land? (Israel was the enemy nation of the Moabites.) And, who benefitted from Ruth's selfless, determined resolve? Of course she did, but so did Naomi, as well as all the Jewish people and ultimately the whole world. Ruth was on a Kingdom assignment, an assignment that culminated in her becoming the great-grandmother of King David – the lineage of Jesus! (Incidentally, the *Encyclopedia Judaica* reports that Orpah, who turned her back on Naomi and remained in Moab, went on to be the great-grandmother of Goliath. Do you see the importance of our choices? Ruth and Orpah/David and Goliath . . .)

There is one additional aspect of Ruth's vow that I believe must be understood. Naomi had no role in keeping any part of that vow. Ruth placed the whole of the vow solely on her own shoulders – no matter what Naomi did or did not do! It was a one-sided vow with all responsibilities for its keeping resting entirely on Ruth. The understanding of this element is absolutely critical.

How many of us have stopped to consider that God's two favorite people groups are His *Chosen* and His *Church*? We are His absolute favorites! (And, please note that all people in the world can fit into one of these two groups.) Yet, there is a despicable, prideful division separating the two that bears the stench of hell and the devil. God loves sweet-smelling aromas rising to His throne, but unfortunately, where Israel and the Jews are concerned, the fragrance given off by many Christians, and some entire churches and denominations, is a far cry from what God genuinely desires.

There is potentially limitless power roaming free on the earth today, which few fail to grasp. It is the untapped resource of a *unified* Israel (all Jews) and the Church (true, evangelical Christians). The possibilities could be earth-shattering. If these two forces were as inextricably woven, as was the relationship Ruth vowed to Naomi, there would be limitless Kingdom work abounding in our world today. No force on earth could stop it.

What if the true Church determinedly *moved*? What if she denounced her arrogance, ignorance and pride (Romans 9, 10 and 11) and embraced God's Chosen People, vowing to love Israel and the Jewish people unconditionally – *till death us do part*? What if the true Church made the same one-sided vow as did Ruth?

What if pastors all over the world prayerfully, reverently and fearfully began embracing the Jewish roots of Christianity? What if the priceless Jewish roots of our faith were embraced and spewed forth from every pulpit of every genuine Church of the Living God all over the face of the earth? What universal impact would that have?

What if pastors *moved* from their comfort zones and began building relationships with area rabbis? What if pastors and rabbis made it a matter of priority to meet for lunch, or coffee, or just simply to meet once a month, working toward bridging that unnecessary, ubiquitous chasm that divides, while gleaning rich truths each from the other?

A starting point might be to hold Passover Seders in our Churches. Jesus observed Passover right before his death, revealing to those present that He was the fulfillment of the Passover promise. Nothing has changed; it is still all about Him. What an incredible teaching tool because every element in the Seder points to the perfect Lamb of God and His shed blood of redemption. What could be more fitting?

Oh, fellow believers, this division has gone on far too long. We have grieved the heart of God in this matter much too deeply. For the Lord's sake, let *us* take that first step, and every step thereafter, if need be. He moved for us; certainly, we can move for Him and for His Kingdom's sake.

I close with the precious words of our Lord.

> *Ye call me Master and Lord: and ye say well; for so I am. If I then, your Lord and Master, have washed your feet; ye also ought to wash one another's feet. For I have given you an example, that ye should do as I have done to you. Verily, verily, I say unto you, The servant is not greater than his lord; neither he that is sent greater than he that sent him.* John 13:13-16.

Prayer: Oh, Father, have exceedingly great mercy and pardon on us! Please prick our hearts in this matter of Jewish-Christian relations. Please give us your understanding. Let us not continue doing things our way any longer. Let us be willing to move wherever and whenever you so choose, especially as relates to your Chosen People. Strip our attitude of superiority and replace it with the very same servant heart that was at home in your Son. "Here am I, Lord;" I yield to your will in this matter, and I commit myself to be totally surrendered and to be used to bridge the great divide between your Chosen and your Church. Let me never again be a divider, but always a repairer of the breaches, I pray in the Perfect and only Name of Jesus, Amen.

Other Books By the Author

Ruth 3,000 Years of Sleeping Prophecy Awakened

Ruth 3,000 Years of Sleeping Prophecy Awakened – Workbook

CPSIA information can be obtained at www.ICGtesting.com
Printed in the USA
LVOW040610281112

309125LV00002B/317/P